the magic of mindful origami

the magic of
mindful origami

declutter your mind
and fold your way to happiness

Samuel Tsang

'You see a blank sheet of paper,
I see infinite possibilities.'

Samuel Tsang

Samuel Tsang is a London-based origami teacher. He has been folding origami since he was a child and teaching professionally since 2003. During that time Sam has introduced origami to thousands of students at public and corporate team-building workshops, working with over 100 companies. Sam also helped organise the Guinness World Record for the largest display of origami elephants, which is now permanently displayed at ZSL Whipsnade Zoo.

Sam creates beautiful bespoke origami bouquets and undertakes commissions for private individuals and businesses. He also runs origami workshops at the Queen of Hoxton club, Drink Shop & Do and with The Indytute in London, all open to beginners. Details are available on his website, www.sesames.co.uk

Born in London, Sam was brought up with traditional Chinese values, a mixture of Buddhism, Taoism and Confucianism. He now lives in West London with his wife, two daughters and a house full of origami.

www.mindfulorigami.com
@mindfulorigami #mindfulorigami

www.mindFOLDness.com
@mindFOLDness #mindFOLDness

bases

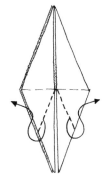

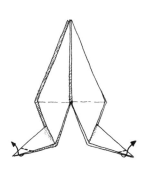

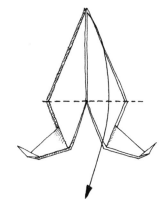

simple models

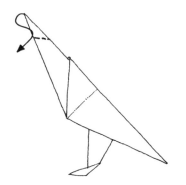

advanced models

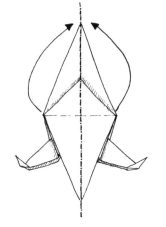

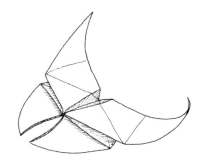

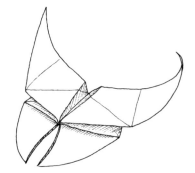

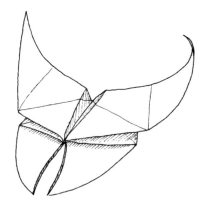

introduction

Do you remember the first time you folded a paper aeroplane? The fun and excitement as you threw it and watched it glide across the room?

Playing children have no worries or doubts – they are absorbed and enraptured by their game, unaware of all around them. And in the same way, although as we become adults we lose our childhood inhibitions and innocent oblivion, certain activities still lend themselves to lifting our spirits or can help alleviate stress and anxiety. Origami is one such pastime.

I have been teaching origami for over a decade and over that time many of my students have commented on how they've found origami not only to be fun and relaxing but also therapeutic, with some even comparing it to meditation. Indeed, I have read references of Zen Buddhists using origami as a form of meditation.

Origami requires you to use your hands, eyes and mind and it will help you learn to focus and concentrate. It will teach you to be methodical, more patient and can help you improve your memory and hand–eye coordination. In short, origami is a path to mindfulness, or as I like to call it, mindFOLDness®.

Many people are apprehensive about trying origami – the models look complicated so naturally they associate it with difficulty. In reality if you can fold a piece of paper in half you can do origami.

It's so easy and indeed, origami is a perfect activity to do with children and it is used in many schools to teach fractions and geometry. There are also therapists using origami as an aid to help children with developmental issues.

In this book, I hope to share the fun and magic of origami with you, and inspire you with the creative and thoughtful process of turning a flat piece of paper into a beautiful piece of art.

origami: the art of folding paper

Origami is the Japanese name for the art of folding paper. Although today origami is most commonly associated with Japan, it is thought that paper folding came to life in different guises in China, Europe and Japan.

Paper was invented in China around 100BC, so it is likely the practice began here, but initially paper was expensive to make and reserved for official and religious ceremonies. Early examples of origami can be seen at traditional Chinese funerals. Paper 'spirit' money was burnt for the deceased to be used in the afterlife. Often the pieces of paper were folded into the shape of a traditional Chinese gold nugget and this tradition is still practised.

It was in Japan that origami grew into the art form that we know today. It is believed that in 6BC Buddhist monks took paper to Japan, where it was used in religious ceremonies. Shinto priests used a ceremonial wand called a 'shide' that was made from folded strips of paper. Initially paper was a rare commodity and origami was reserved for these ceremonial purposes: origami butterflies were used to decorate sake bottles during Japanese weddings, for example. However, as the process of making paper became more industrialised it became cheaper and more widely available, used for printing books and teaching children to read and write.

It is not known how origami originated but I like to think that it was a child who first discovered that they could fold paper from their school textbook into a bird or butterfly.

The first reference to origami in print was in the eighteenth century – in the origami book *Hiden Senbazuru Orikata (The Secret of Folding One Thousand Cranes)*, published in 1797. But origami only started to become a popular hobby outside of Japan in the twentieth century. Before the printed press, the instructions for making the models were handed down from parent to child. But in 1954 a Japanese origamist named Akira Yoshizawa created a set of instructional diagrams using arrows and dotted lines to denote the different folds required to create a model. This instruction set has now become the standard for all origami models.

With the advent of the computer in the 1970s some mathematicians and scientists started to study the mathematical principles behind origami. Like a lot of scientific research, what was done out of academic curiosity has led to some unexpected uses. They discovered that the principles behind origami could be used to fold large objects into smaller, more compact shapes and this knowledge has since been used in satellite solar panelling, car air bags and medical heart stents.

The number of unique traditional origami models is actually quite limited, numbering fewer than 100 but in the last two decades the number of origami designs has exploded with the creation of computer programs that can actually create new origami designs. The popularity of origami is still growing every year.

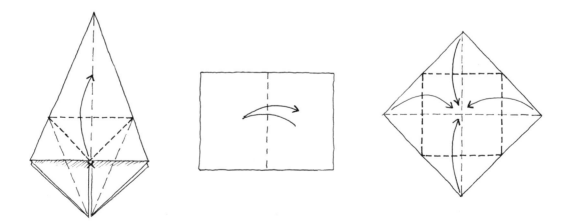

perspective, persistence, patience and practice

I have taught origami to complete beginners for over 10 years now. When I first started teaching workshops I would sometimes encounter individuals who became frustrated with origami. I even had a couple of people walk out of a workshop because they had become so exasperated with it. I wondered what had caused these individuals to have what, in my mind, was quite an extreme reaction. After all, for most people, origami is an inconsequential skill. I thought about these people and I came to the conclusion that they were frustrated because they were not understanding the instructions I was giving them, and I believed that this was a failing in my teaching skills and ability to convey the instructions simply enough for everyone to understand. This was what was causing them to be unsatisfied and unfulfilled by their experience of origami and ultimately to give up.

The problem with that conclusion is that in a class of 40 or 50 people of all ages, backgrounds and abilities the majority grasped the concept and successfully completed the models. Even more importantly, there were other individuals who also failed to complete the model yet did not leave or seem to get even slightly frustrated.

I pondered this for a long time until I decided to ask one individual why they were getting frustrated. Their response was, 'I feel stupid that I can't grasp such a simple skill.'

One of the greatest problems with our generation is our belief that we should be able to grasp any concept or skill on our first try, so failure to be able to do this, in turn, makes us a failure. Is it reasonable or rational to believe that we should be able to understand every concept or grasp a new skill on our first exposure to it?

If you find that you are unable to do something the first time, all it means is that your mind has never encountered that problem before and as such you have not learned the skills to deal with it.

This may seem like cold comfort for some but even the simplest skills such as reading and writing take us years of practice to perfect.

Origami seems simple. Its primary skill is the ability to fold a piece of paper in half. But in the same sense the fundamental skill of being a concert pianist is the ability to press a piano key. It would, of course, be absurd to think that after just one piano lesson you could replicate the performance of a concert pianist. You realise that to be a proficient pianist requires more than to be able to press a piano key, it requires the knowledge and skill to read music, to have the hand–eye coordination to play, and it takes countless months of practice to become even mildly proficient at the piano let alone be a concert pianist. The same is true for origami. The fundamental skill is to be able to fold paper but you also need to learn to read and understand the instructions, have hand–eye coordination, spatial reasoning to know where to make folds, and enough practice to be able to make the fold with precision and accuracy.

The models in this book are split into different levels of difficulty and gradually get more difficult as you progress through the book. You should be able to complete the simplest models on the first or second try. The more complex of the simple models might take you three or four attempts and the advanced models might take you many more (the most difficult model – the swan – is for people who are very experienced in origami and could take months for you to learn).

You should view origami as a puzzle, something that you may not be able to solve on the first, second or even the tenth try. But as with a puzzle there is immense satisfaction when you crack it! So when you are stuck, remember that failure to complete a model does not make you a failure, it just means you have not practised enough. If you find you get frustrated while folding, put the model away and come back to it later, maybe even weeks later. If you are still really stuck and want more immediate help to avoid further frustration, you can visit my website (www. mindfulorigami.com) where there are videos to help you. So, I will leave you with my four P's for mindful origami (these are also valid for life in general!):

perspective – don't take it too seriously.

persistence – you only fail when you give up.

patience – any skill will take time to learn.

practice – only with continuous practice will you become proficient.

the path to mindfulness

In today's world, we live in a relentless 'rushed' state. From the moment we wake we hurry to get to work, swallow our lunch to get back to our desks, and power through our tasks to meet our deadlines. We work long hours, multitask each day and respond to a constant stream of queries using multiple devices.

When we are constantly rushed, our bodies become tired. When our minds are rushed, we become forgetful, unsure and anxious. We are constantly trying to reach the next checkpoint and we are rarely able to appreciate the present moment.

The accepted definition of mindfulness is to be aware of the present moment without judgement. To be mindful is simply to be conscious and truly aware of your own thoughts, feelings and surroundings.

It has also been described as the process of quieting the mind to free it of distracting thoughts, or as the opposite of 'multitasking' – focusing your mind on the current thought or activity you are engaged in.

We are often so busy trying to complete the next task that we forget to enjoy what we are doing in the present. By living in the present moment you can start to appreciate and enjoy the life you are living and be free of stress, anxiety and fear. By learning to be mindful it will help you to stop negative thoughts, reduce your stress and anxieties. Indeed, mindfulness training has now been recognised by the National Health Service in the UK as a way to reduce stress and anxiety and promote mental well-being.

Mindfulness is not happiness but it is directly connected to it. It is not a quick fix to all the problems in your life, it is not even a slow fix, it is just a signpost indicating a possible pathway to happiness.

Being mindful is to know where you are right now, but it is up to you to find the correct path to where you want to be. Mindfulness is the compass or map; you still have to climb those mountains yourself.

There is no wrong or right way to practise mindfulness. Being mindful is not something measurable, it is a process to become aware of your true self. It will help you identify the cause of stress and sadness in your life and once identified you can either try to fix the problem, avoid its causes or learn to manage and accept them.

You will also become aware of what truly makes you happy and not the expectations that have been drummed into you by society.

Two burgeoning trends have struck me over the past decade. The first is the increasing popularity of mindful activities such as yoga, pilates, tai chi and meditation. The second has been the huge resurgence in arts and crafts. I believe that both are a direct response to people needing to calm their minds and slow their lives. Many of us have office jobs where we sit in front of a computer screen all day. We tap away at a keyboard, creating documents and spreadsheets that might be looked at once and never seen again. In the digital world, our work is virtual – fleeting – and we are often just a small cog in a big machine. We can rarely see the physical fruits of our labour. All this has led to a desire, a need even, for a creative outlet; we want to be able to make something real, something we can touch. Origami is a fusing of both these needs: creating some calm and producing something tangible. When you are learning to fold, your hands, eyes and mind are fully focused on the task of creation and you are able to ignore external distractions. Through origami you can find calm and be in the moment.

'A journey of a thousand miles begins with a single step.'
Lao Tzu

mindful origami

Origami is simply the act of folding paper, but it is the intent and thought behind this action that determines whether it is positive or negative and therefore whether it is mindful or not. Any activity can be done mindfully and this is the ultimate goal – to be mindful at all times; to be aware and enjoy your life.

Mindful origami uses the creative process of folding a model as a meditative aid and the models you make are a physical manifestation of your desire to be more mindful and hopefully happier.

In practising mindful origami it is important to remember that the meditation and the learning process are more important than completing the origami model. Your intent should be to meditate on a theme and to learn the process of origami. Completion of a model is just an aid in the process. It is a piece of folded paper; there are no consequences if you do not complete the model.

There are two stages to becoming mindful during your origami practice. The first stage is to slip into a calm frame of mind, where your attention is focused on the piece of paper in your hands. During this phase you will not be meditating but you will be concentrating and learning. When you are in learning mode your mind is focusing on the present moment and will naturally block out all your distracting thoughts.

The second stage of mindful origami is the meditation. I have folded tens of thousands of models and there are some models that I can fold without thinking. When I am crafting these models I am calm and can allow my thoughts to wander. Sometimes my mind will start to crystallise a thought or recall a memory, person or feeling associated with the model. When you have learned to fold your model by heart, without referring to the illustrations, you will be able to reflect on its meaning – or theme – and its effect or presence in your own life. For instance, I designed an origami rose for my wife and named it the Carmen Curler rose (see page 99). Curler is the method by which the rose is created – it is curled. This model takes more than 20 minutes to fold and as I fold this model I think only of Carmen in a calm and positive light; I reflect on our life together and recall all my happy memories with her.

Ask yourself, when was the last time that you sat and thought about one person in a quiet concentrated way? More often than not our minds are so busy that thoughts for our loved ones are only fleeting and are quickly replaced with the daily task list we have to work through. But if we regularly take time to think about the people we love in positive contemplation we will find that we appreciate them more. We become grateful for their presence in our life and we are more aware of treating them with the care, attention and understanding that they deserve. This in turn enables us to nurture and strengthen our relationships and increase our own happiness. The practise is traditionally called a 'Loving Kindness' meditation.

Mindful origami is the use of origami as a meditation aid – it allows us to sit and create a piece of art but it also allows us to start meditating without realising we are doing it. Like yoga and pilates, where the more advanced poses take time to learn and you may not manage them on the first attempt, so it is with the origami models you will be folding. When you look at your model do not judge it or judge yourself, there is no perfection. If you are stuck on a difficult step, do not be frustrated. Take a breath and try again. If the model doesn't look like the picture, do not be upset; no two flowers are identical. The learning is all part of the process of becoming mindful. And like yoga or meditation the benefits of origami only become apparent if you practise regularly. As you become more accomplished and proficient at folding, you will soon be able to enter a mindful state as you create your models. While meditating you may not crystallise any thoughts or draw any conclusions; true understanding takes time and effort. Through repeated practice you will learn to perfect the model and once you have, you will be able to focus your mind on the meditation and eventually come to a conclusion.

'Be happy in the moment, that's enough.
Each moment is all we need, not more.'
Mother Teresa

about this book

In this book I have chosen 16 origami models for you to work through: 14 traditional models and two of my own design (the rose and the swan). The models start from the simplest and progressively become more challenging. I suggest you work methodically through the book from start to finish. If you are new to origami do not attempt the hardest models first as this will just frustrate you. You must learn to walk before you can run.

Work calmly and steadily through each step. Check the step you have just done before moving on. As you fold, study the paper, the lines and the colours. Feel the texture of the paper between your fingers and notice the sound as you make each crease.

Each model within the book has a suggested theme to reflect on. Try to relate each model to an associated thought, memory or feeling, though note that the themes are merely my suggestion so allow your thoughts to drift and wander; mindful origami is an exploration of your own meditations and feelings. If you find that something is consuming your attention, stop folding and let it take its natural progression through your mind. Once that thought or feeling has subsided, continue with your origami.

When you complete the model reflect on what thoughts and feelings you had while folding. Certain models have spaces at the end of each chapter where you can write down these thoughts and build up a log of your meditations. Or, if you have crystallised a particular thought, aim or idea, write it on the actual model itself and hang it somewhere prominent. By placing the models somewhere you can see them every day they will act as visual reminders of your intentions. I would also encourage you to offer your models to others. Give them freely to people you know as well as to complete strangers without expecting anything in return. Think of this as a mindful act: making others happy with a small gesture of kindness.

Finally, be kind to yourself. The majority of models within this book are for complete beginners and will not take long to grasp; the last few are more complicated. If you find you are stuck on a particular step, stop folding, but continue meditating on the theme and topic. When you are ready, pick up the model and slowly turn the model, noting the position of each crease and edge. Read the step you are stuck on and try again. Remember, the learning is just as mindful as the folding.

paper

Origami can be folded from any paper available. The vast majority of origami is folded from square paper but there are many examples of it being folded from rectangular, pentagonal, hexagonal and octagonal shaped paper. The boat and shirt models in this book, for example, can be folded from a standard A4 sheet and the ring and star are folded from paper strips that you will need to cut to size. For 11 of the remaining models there are pull-out pages at the back of the book. These pages have crease patterns printed on them, which show where all the fold lines are on each model (there is no pattern for the rose as it's made from multiples, and duplicates of the tortoise and swan as they're the most complicated). By using these crease patterns and following the instructions in the book you should be able to complete the models more easily.

The crease patterns give you another outlet for artistic expression: colour them in and see what your subconscious reveals. You can also print additional crease patterns by visiting www.mindfulorigami.com and downloading the free pdf files.

Origami paper can also be found in most art stores and online. It comes in many sizes, colours and textures. The smallest origami crane models measure 0.1mm and have to be viewed under a microscope, while the largest is the size of a football field. The most common origami paper size is 15 x 15cm and this format comes in the largest range of patterns, colours and textures. This is the most popular size as it is the most easily manipulated and folded – not so small that it becomes difficult to fold by adults and not too large so that it becomes unwieldy to fold.

The paper weight and thickness is usually between 60 and 80gsm but any paper can be folded as long as it can hold a crease (though I do not recommend folding paper that is thicker than 140gsm as it is difficult to crease due to its stiffness and also the paper tends to rip along the fold lines).

If you are new to origami then you can just use standard A4 paper and cut it into a square to fold. Then after you have mastered a few of the basic models why not treat yourself and purchase some traditional coloured origami papers.

14 steps to mindFOLDness®

1   Wash your hands. You can consider this a cleansing ritual but in reality it is just to avoid leaving greasy fingerprints on your finished model.

2   Sit in a comfortable and quiet place with a table. Relax your body and clear your mind of the daily grind.

3   Read the instructions for each model thoroughly before beginning to fold.

4   Think about the theme of the story. Close your eyes if it helps. Try to recall a memory of your own that relates to the theme.

5   Fold when you are ready, following each step carefully.

6   Meditate. Let your thoughts drift and wander.

7   Consciously use your senses while folding. See the lines and shadows, feel the texture of the paper, hear the sounds as you fold.

8   Stop and take a breather to check you have folded each step correctly.

9   Continue folding until the model is complete.

10 Now pick up the model and appreciate what you have created. Well done!

11 Each time you fold and meditate keep a log of your thoughts and feelings in the space at the end of each chapter. If along the way you have crystallised any thoughts, write them on the model itself.

12 Place or hang the model somewhere prominent. Whenever you look at this model you will associate it with that thought or memory.

13 Repeat the model until you can make it by heart and then you will be able to purely focus on the meditation.

14 Carry out mindful acts of kindness by giving away your completed models without expecting anything in return.

instruction symbols: dashes, dots and arrows

Set out in this section are the basic instruction symbols for the folds used throughout the book. If you're new to origami, you will need to read and practise each one of these folds before beginning any of the models. Think of them as warm-up exercises.

valley fold

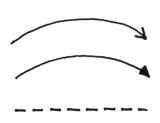 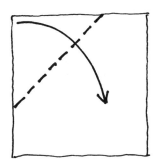 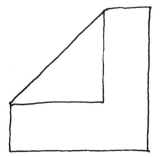

This is the most basic origami fold, represented by a dash line and an arrow to indicate the direction of the fold. Fold the paper towards you and crease along the line. If you look at the crease sideways it will look like an upside-down 'V'.

mountain fold

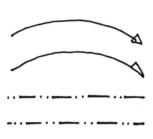 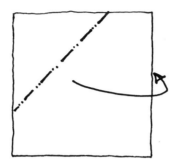 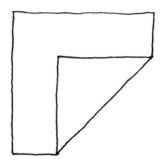

A mountain fold is indicated by a dash-dot-dot-dash line and an arrow to indicate the direction of the fold. You fold the paper so that it is folded behind itself (or away from you), which creates a crease that looks like the peak of a mountain.

fold and unfold

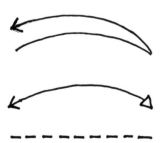 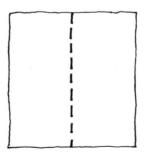 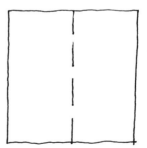

This symbol means that the paper is folded in half, then unfolded. This results in a crease line that can be used later.

turn over (and an invisible line)

This symbol indicates you have to turn the model over. The dotted line indicates the edge of the paper that is now underneath.

rotate

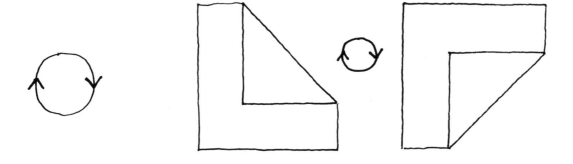

This symbol is the instruction for rotating the paper. The arrow indicates whether to rotate clockwise or anticlockwise and a number in the middle will indicate if you should rotate by 90 or 180 degrees.

inside reverse fold

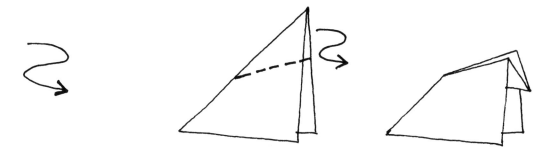

To make an inside reverse fold you have to push a fold in on itself. The easiest way to make an inside reverse fold is to make a valley fold on the dotted line first, then unfold it and push the fold in on itself.

outside reverse fold

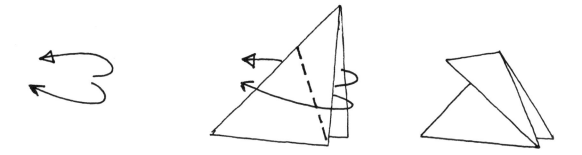

To make an outside reverse fold you have to pull the two edges indicated over the paper. Imagine it as if you were pulling the hood of your raincoat over your head. As with an inside reverse fold, the easiest way to make an outside reverse fold is to make a valley fold on the dotted line, then unfold it and use the crease to make the outside fold.

fold point to point

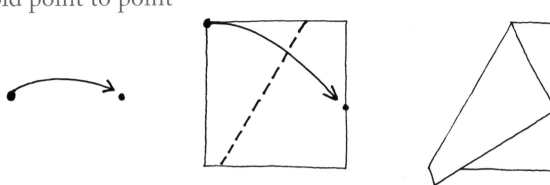

This symbol means that you should fold along the dotted line so that the two points indicated lie on top of each other.

pleat (or accordion) fold

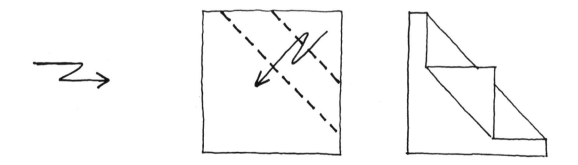

As it sounds, a pleat, or accordion, fold indicates that you need to make two folds. The first is a valley fold and the second a mountain fold so that you end up with a pleat as shown.

open

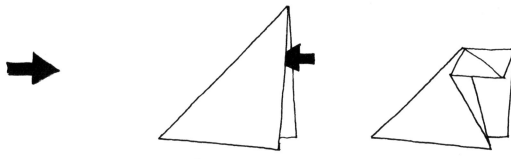

An arrow like this means that you need to open out the model by separating the two edges of the paper where indicated. Usually when you see this symbol there are some pre-made creases on the model that will cause it to open along natural lines and hold its shape.

pull

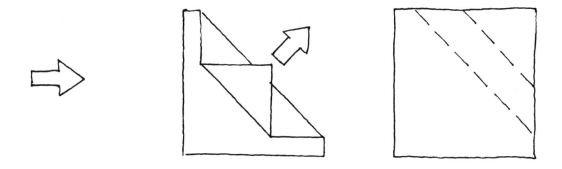

Simply pull at the point indicated.

inside crimp

 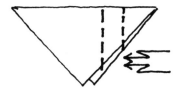 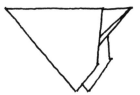

This symbol indicates that you have to make folds through both layers and then you have to sink one fold inside the other. Another way to explain it would be to make an inside reverse fold and then another inside reverse fold in the other direction. Essentially, you are pleating the section indicated.

outside crimp

 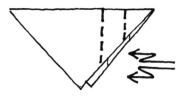 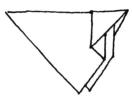

An inside crimp in reverse, so an outside reverse fold and then another outside reverse fold in the other direction. Again, you have to make folds through both layers.

sink

  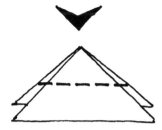

A sink fold tucks part of a model inside the other. The easiest way to make sink folds is to fold and unfold right through all the layers on the dotted line, then gently tuck the point indicated down into the section inside.

inflate

 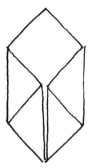 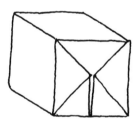

This symbol means you have to blow into the hole to inflate the model. Before inflating, make sure you have a dry mouth so you don't wet and damage your model. Also don't hold the model too tightly when blowing as this will prevent it from inflating fully.

bases

The 'bases' provided in this section are the most basic form of origami and the starting point for a vast number of models. Think of them as the foundation of the model you are folding. By learning to fold these bases correctly and accurately you will enable yourself to fold complex models without frustration. If the base is not accurate then later fold lines and edges will be out of alignment and you will find it difficult to complete the model. You must learn to walk before you can run so as with the instruction symbols, do please practise all these bases before starting any of the models.

make a square from rectangular paper

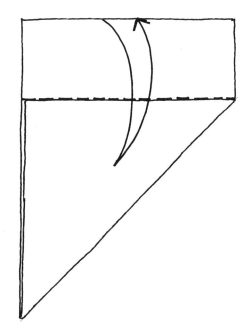

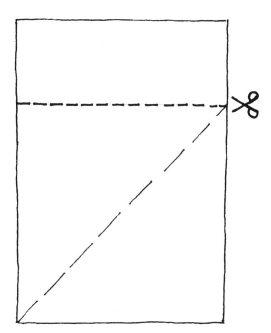

step 1

Valley fold and unfold along the dotted line – the bottom right corner should meet the left edge.

step 2

Cut along the small dotted line and you will have a perfect square.

square base

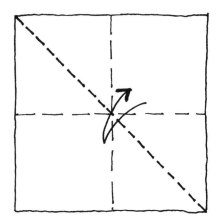

step 2

Fold and unfold along one of the diagonals. Make the fold from corner to corner trying to be as neat and accurate as possible.

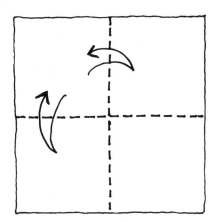

step 1

First you will need to fold some squares. Start with the white side of the paper facing you. Fold and unfold along the horizontal and vertical dotted lines.

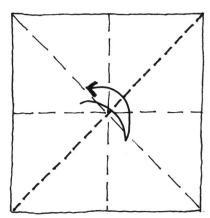

step 3

Turn the paper over so that the coloured side is facing you. Fold and unfold the other diagonal, again corner to corner.

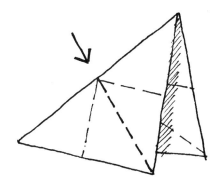

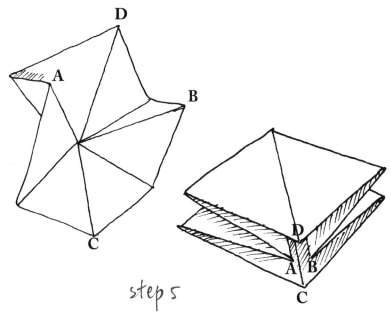

step 4

Turn it back over to the white side. The model should stand up like a wigwam. You are now going to pack away the wigwam by collapsing it. Push down on the centre point as indicated to begin to flatten the model.

step 5

Two of the corners (A and B) will start to pop up – bring them together. Then bring the other two corners (C and D) together and the whole model will collapse down into the square base.

point

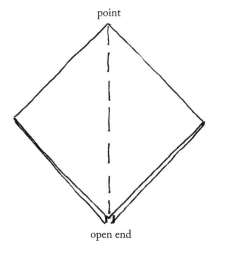

open end

The vast majority of basic origami models begin with the square or the triangle base (see page 34) so I would urge you to become familiar with this base before progressing to the models. Note that it has a point and open end. Also note that it has four branches. Origami is all about symmetry and whatever fold you make on one branch will normally have to be repeated on the three other branches.

triangle base

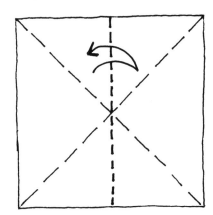

step 2

Valley fold and unfold along the vertical line.

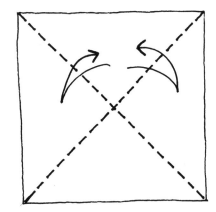

step 1

Start with the white side of the paper facing you.
Valley fold both diagonals, corner to corner.

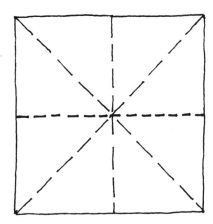

step 3

Turn the paper over on to the coloured side and
valley fold along the horizontal line.

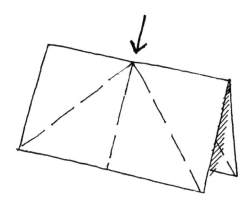

step 4

Turn the model back over on to the white side; it should stand up like a tent. You are now going to pack your tent away by collapsing it. Push down on the point as indicated to begin to flatten it.

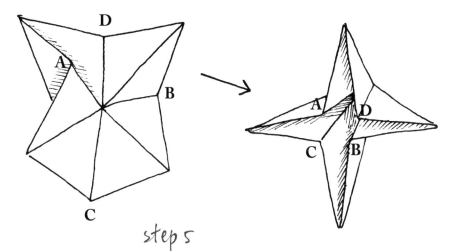

step 5

As you push down, bring points A and B together. Then bring C and D together. Flatten the model and it will collapse into the triangle base.

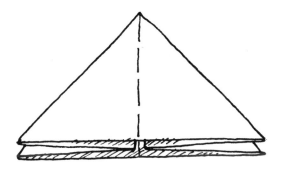

Become familiar with this base before progressing to the models.

bird base

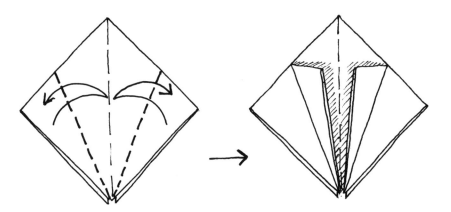

step 1

Start by folding a square base (see page 32).
Valley fold the two upper layers then unfold.

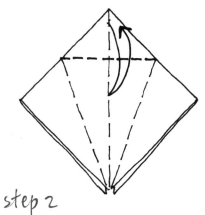

step 2

Valley fold the top triangle down.

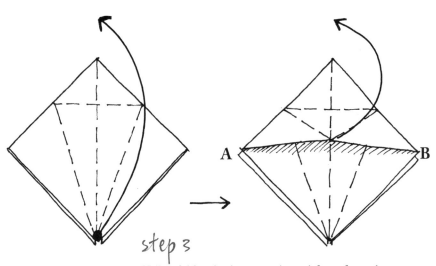

step 3

Valley fold only the upper layer, lifting from the
point indicated. As you lift, it will pivot along the
dotted line and points A and B will move towards
each other.

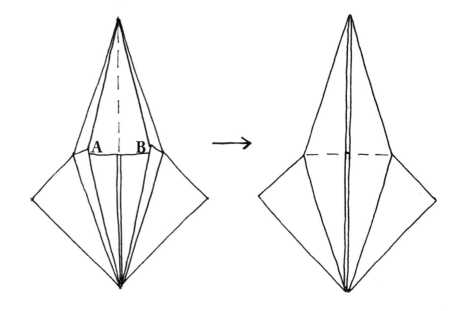

step 4

Push points A and B down towards the centre line and flatten the model. Then turn over and repeat steps 1–4 on the other side. You will end up with a flat diamond shape. Steps 3 and 4 are also known as a petal fold.

This is called a bird base because it is the starting point for many bird models. If you look at it from the side, you will see it has a triangle hump in the middle which is the body of the bird. It has two parallel wings and what look like two legs which often become the head and the tail of the bird.

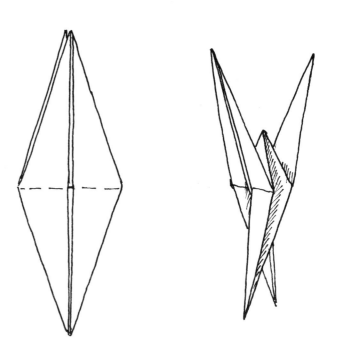

fish base

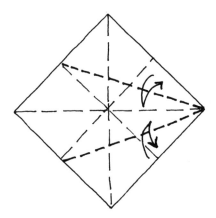

step 2

Valley fold and unfold along the small dotted lines.

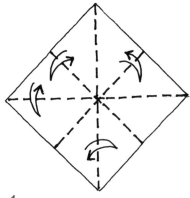

step 1

Valley fold and unfold along each dotted line.

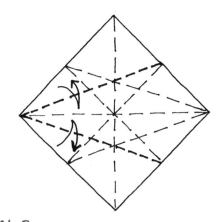

step 3

Valley fold and unfold along the small dotted lines.

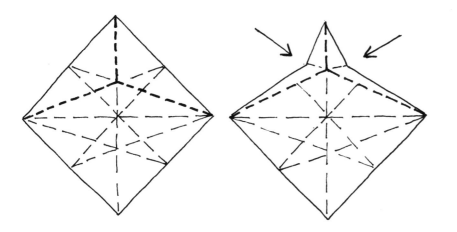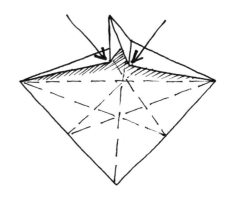

step 4

Valley fold on the dotted lines. As you fold, push down on the edges where indicated to flatten the model.

step 5

Push down at the points indicated – the edges will flatten and you will form a triangular fin. Now repeat the last two steps on the bottom half.

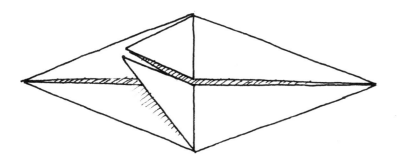

This is called a fish base because it is the starting point for many fish models. You will notice it has two triangle flaps on each side that can be used as fins.

Please note that the bird and fish bases are just the recognised names given to them by the origami community. Any base can be folded into infinite shapes, objects and animals.

'Shape clay into a vessel; it is the space within that makes it useful.'
Lao Tzu

box 箱

As Lao Tzu tells us, it is a vessel's emptiness that makes it valuable to us. A cup is only useful if it can hold water; a house if it has space to live in; a mind if it is clear to have thoughts; and a heart if it has room for love.

Our heart and mind are like boxes: when we are born they are empty but as we grow they slowly fill with emotions and memories. As the boxes fill, there may be times when the number of negative thoughts exceeds our positive and happy memories. Negativity adds no value to our lives so to be happier and more fulfilled we need to de-clutter – to empty part of the box again and leave space for joy and positivity.

As you fold your box, think about what fills your heart and your mind. What truly needs to be there? Which memories and emotions make your life happier? What thoughts and memories should be taken out of that box?

reflections

This simple box model was the mystery crease pattern that was included at the end of my first book, *The Book of Mindful Origami*. On the back of that crease pattern I had written 'make of it what you will'. The quote refers to our lives: we all make what we will to create our own life. My hope was that the pattern would encourage readers to experiment and explore origami outside of a book and an instruction set. Perhaps there would be someone that managed to fold something completely different and new using this crease pattern? Although by practising origami you are creating something wonderful to hold and to keep; true creativity lies in creating something new.

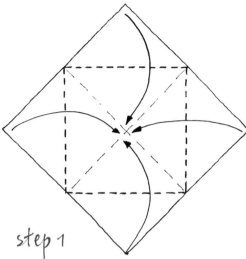 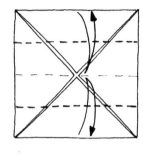 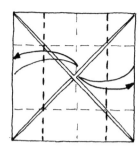

step 1

Start with an open square base (see page 32) and fold all four corners into the centre.

step 2

Valley fold and unfold along the dotted lines; the top and bottom edges should meet in the middle.

step 3

Valley fold and unfold along the dotted lines; the left and right edges should meet in the middle.

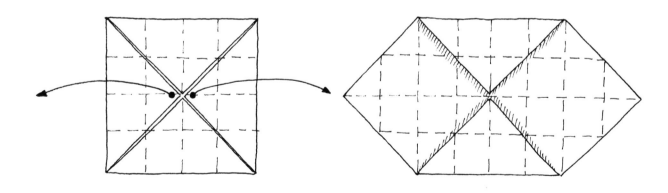

step 4

Pull on the left and right corners indicated by the dots and open them out.

box **41**

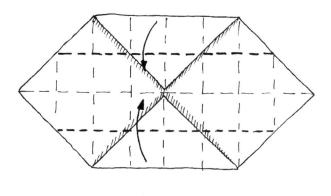

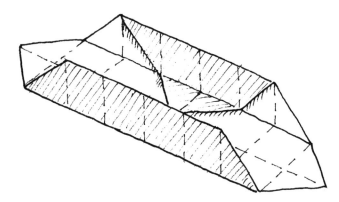

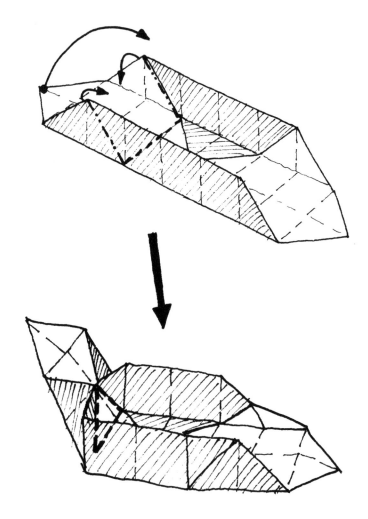

step 5

Fold along the two horizontal dotted lines so that the top and bottom edge are standing upright to form the sides of the box. From the side the model should look U-shaped.

step 6

Lift the corner point upward using the dotted line as the pivot; this will start to create the third wall of the box.

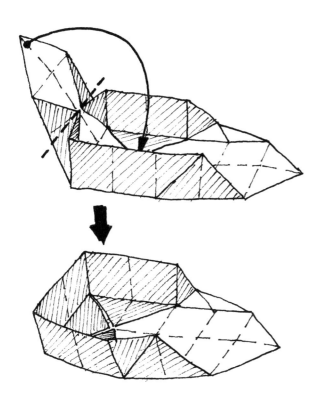

step 7

Valley fold the corner down along the dotted line to form the third wall of the box. Repeat these steps on the other side to complete the last wall of the box.

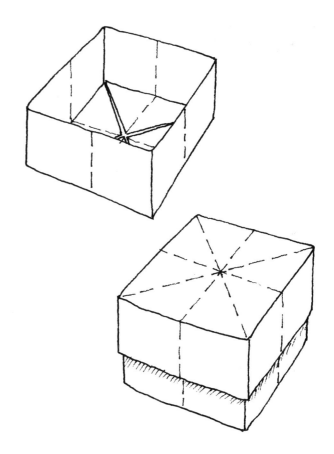

This box is a great example of practical origami. If you fold another box from a piece of paper that is about 5mm larger you can use it as a lid, then use the box as a gift box or for storing trinkets and even origami paper. Alternatively, if you fold boxes out of aluminium foil or parchment paper you can use them as baking ramekins.

box 43

boat 船

Have you ever taken a boat ride for enjoyment? Perhaps you've rowed a boat around a lake, sailed out to sea on a yacht, or have even taken a cruise? What was the aim of that trip? Was it to get to the final destination as quickly as possible? Or was it to enjoy the journey?

Mindfulness is about appreciating and enjoying the present moment. Life is a journey to be savoured, not rushed, yet one of the main problems with modern society is that everyone seems to lack patience. We sigh with exasperation when our train is a few minutes late; we beep our horn at the car that doesn't move the instant the light goes green; we get annoyed when a website doesn't load instantly.

As you fold your boat try to remember the last time you lost your patience with someone or something. Did losing your patience improve that situation? Or did your impatience cause you further problems or delay? With impatience come errors and misunderstanding so by learning to be more patient we help maintain our own peace of mind and help reduce misinterpretation and conflict.

Origami is a practice in patience. Your aim is not to complete the model as quickly as possible, it is to complete it with appreciation and enjoyment and to learn from the experience.

reflections

As a child I remember making paper boats, setting them afloat on a river and watching them drift out of sight. I always wondered if it would be possible to make a real origami boat that I could sail in but as I grew older I dismissed this as a ridiculous idea. Then in January 2015 I read an article recounting how pupils at Tottenham UTC school in North London had actually made one as a contribution to 'The Big Bang Fair', a fair promoting and celebrating science, technology, engineering and maths (STEM) for young people in the UK. Their boat was based on the model you'll make on these pages, used 100kg of paper and measured over 3 metres long. It succeeded in carrying an adult across a lake and stayed afloat for more than two hours.

For this model you will need a rectangular piece of paper – an A4 sheet is perfect.

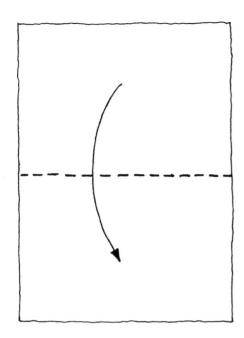

step 1

Valley fold along the dotted line.

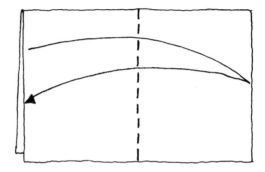

step 2

Valley fold and unfold along the dotted line.

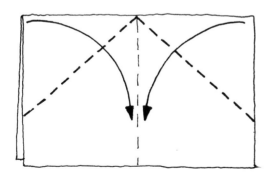

step 3

Valley fold along the diagonal dotted lines so that
the corners meet in the middle.

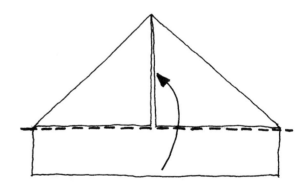

step 4

Valley fold only the top layer upwards along the
dotted line. Turn over and repeat on the other side.

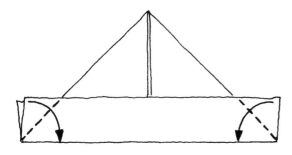

step 5

Valley fold the corners down along the dotted lines
(you only need to do this on one side).

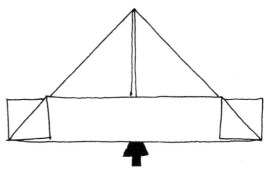

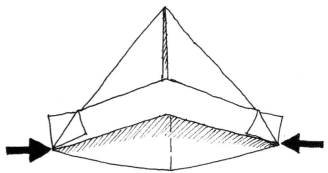

step 6

Open up the model as indicated by the arrow, then push the
left and right corners together until the model is flattened.

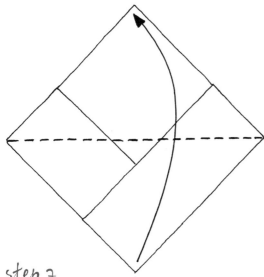

step 7

Valley fold the bottom corner up to the top and
repeat on the back.

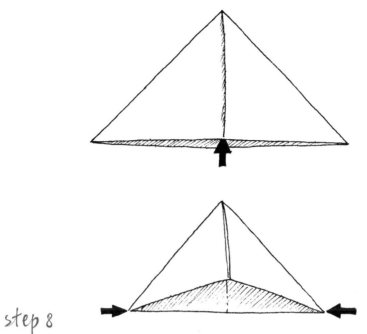

step 8

Open up the model as indicated by the arrow, then push the left and right corners together until the model is flattened.

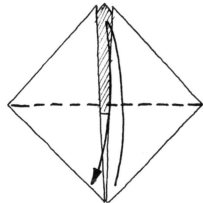

step 9

Valley fold and unfold along the dotted line, then repeat on the back.

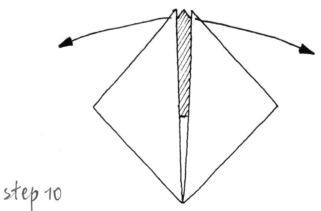

step 10

Pull the two points outwards and the boat will be formed.

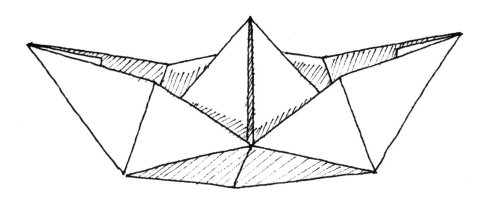

Write the words 'be patient' on both sides of this boat and then hang it somewhere to remind yourself to slow down and enjoy the present moment.

'Your own self-realisation is the greatest service you can render the world.'
Ramana Maharshi

shirt 襯衫

What clothes are you wearing right now? What is the value of those clothes and how important are they to you? In simple terms our clothes protect us from the elements. Without appropriate clothing we would be burned by the sun or frozen by the wind and rain. But clothes are often more than just a protective layer. In nature, animals display colourful patterns and plumage to attract a mate or to ward off predators; their markings can also show membership to a group or reflect their social rank.

Clothes can make us feel good; they can convey our sense of status, wealth and identity. Psychologists believe that the clothing we choose to wear is often used as a form of communication; it is a declaration of how we want others to perceive and identify us and ultimately how we want to see ourselves – our 'social skin'.

Think about your clothing. Is it conveying a message? Ask yourself if that message is representative of your true self. Often the message we transmit may not be representative of the person underneath the clothes; it is a voice telling us we should act and look a certain way as it will either impress others or protect us from others. It is who we think we should be; but it is not who we really are. Say to yourself, 'who are you?'.

Are you your clothes? What happens if they are taken away and you are naked? Are you your body? What if we remove your body? Are you nothing? Or are you the thoughts, knowledge and emotions within your mind? What if we remove even those, then what is left?

What is left is your consciousness, your awareness and your spirit – your true self. By realising that your possessions, clothes, body, job and knowledge are not really you, you become aware that events and people that have hurt you in the past didn't really hurt you, they hurt your ego. Your ego is not the real you. And in knowing this you are able to let go of hurt and pain and realise that your spirit is actually invulnerable to any form of insult or attack.

For this model you will need a rectangular piece of paper – an A4 sheet is perfect.

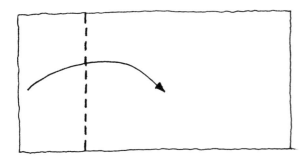

step 1

Valley fold along the dotted line; the left edge should end up in the middle of the paper, approximately.

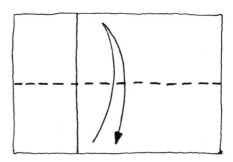

step 2

Valley fold and unfold along the dotted line to make a horizontal crease in the middle.

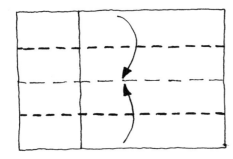

step 3

Valley fold along the dotted lines so that the top and bottom edges meet in the middle.

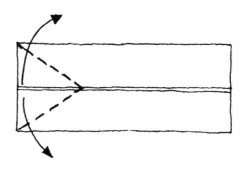

step 4

Valley fold along the two diagonal lines to form the sleeves of the shirt.

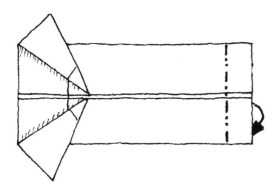

step 5

Mountain fold along the dotted line to create the shirt's collar.

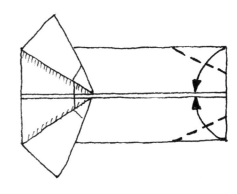

step 6

Valley fold along the two diagonal lines to form the lapels of the collar; the two corners should meet in the middle.

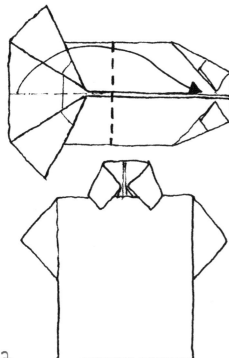

step 7

Valley fold along the dotted line and tuck the edge of the paper under the collar lapels to lock the shirt in place.

You can also fold a shirt from a bank note. Try making waiting staff in a restaurant smile by giving them a folded shirt as a tip. Or make gifting children money a little more fun – you're guaranteed to get a giggle.

'Prejudice is a burden that confuses the past, threatens the future and renders the present inaccessible.'
Maya Angelou

duck 鴨

Did your parents tell you bedtime stories when you were young? Children's stories are the stuff of adventure and magic, created to entertain and enchant. Yet many traditional stories – fables and fairy tales – were also conceived to educate young minds; they contain a moral which we hope to use to instil a sense of right and wrong in our children.

Hans Christian Andersen's tale of the ugly duckling tells of a duckling that was born differently from his siblings. He was grey, larger and uglier and because of this physical difference he was ostracised by his family and community. After a cold, lonely winter, hiding in caves to shelter from the partly frozen lake, the ugly duckling emerges in spring to see his reflection in the water and discover that he is in fact a swan. The story is told to children to teach them that we may start out in life as an ugly duckling and that others may try to hurt us but that if we endure we will all grow into beautiful swans. There is also the lesson that we should not treat others badly just because they look different to us.

To be prejudiced is to prejudge someone before knowing them. As young children, our minds are blank canvasses: we do not have prejudices and we do not discriminate just because people look different to us. We are taught that we should treat all people with equal respect and kindness, yet many of us end up adopting prejudices as we grow. These are learned through the people in our lives; some are taught to us by our families and some we pick up through our interactions with others.

As you crease your duckling, reflect on whether you have ever been a victim of prejudice, or have you shown prejudice towards others? Can you pinpoint the root of that prejudice and can you justify it? Prejudice is born through ignorance and it is the seed of hatred and conflict. By eliminating our prejudices we remove a cause of hatred and negative emotion in our lives.

reflections

I have two young daughters and I often make origami animals for them to play with. If you have children why not make a few ducks and the swan (see page 106) and use them as storytelling props.

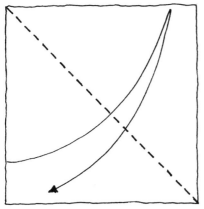

step 1

Valley fold and unfold along the dotted line.

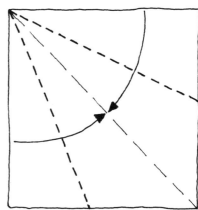

step 2

Valley fold along the dotted lines.

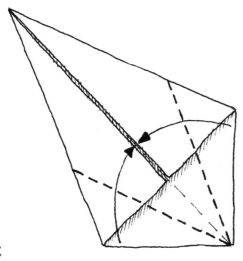

step 3

Valley fold along the dotted lines. Turn the model over.

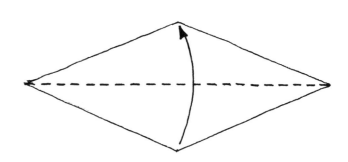

step 4

Valley fold along the dotted line.

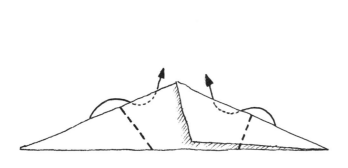

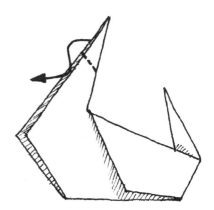

step 5

Inside reverse fold along the dotted lines to make the head and tail.

step 6

Inside reverse fold along the dotted line to make the beak.

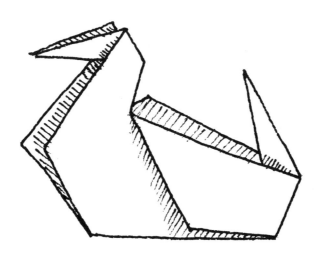

'All men know the use of the useful, but nobody knows the use of the useless.'
Zhuangzi

balloon 氣 球

The origami balloon, or waterbomb model, as it is also known, is a very popular playground toy. The rounded cube form is one of the few origami models that needs to be inflated but also folds flat.

Origami is often seen as a fun and interesting craft but ultimately a pointless and useless skill. However, the techniques in origami have been replicated and used in cutting-edge developments in science and engineering. This particular model was the inspiration for a collapsible cardiac stent, a tube used to keep a collapsed or blocked artery open and restore blood flow.

In 2003, Zhong You and Kaori Kuribayashi designed a stent with a collapsed width of 12mm, which was then threaded into a blood vessel, manoeuvred into position in the blocked artery, and expanded to a width of 23mm to open up the artery and restore blood flow.

As you fold then blow into your balloon, consider the fact that a seemingly useless paper toy inspired scientists to create a potentially live-saving device. What talents and skills do you have? Do you have a skill that may seem pointless? Maybe with the right application it too could be practical and valuable? We value what we believe to be useful and disregard things that we believe are useless yet everything has a value and anything can be inspirational. What use is a beautiful sunset? Except to make our hearts soar?

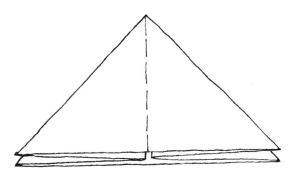

step 1

Start with a triangle base (see page 34).

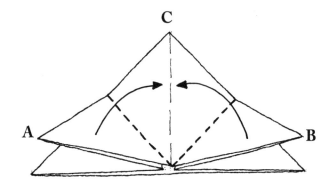

step 2

Working just on the top layer, valley fold points A and B up to meet the centre point C. Turn over and repeat on the other side.

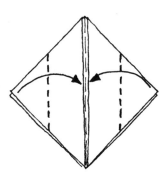

step 3

Valley fold along the dotted lines; the two corners will meet in the middle. Turn over and repeat on the back.

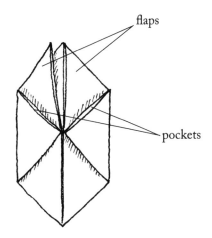

step 4

Note the position of the pockets and flaps.

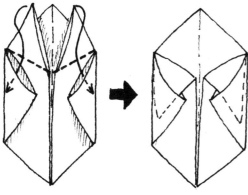

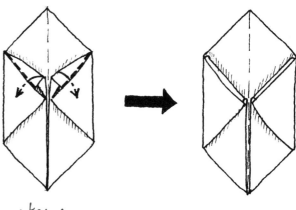

step 5

Bend and tuck the flaps into the pockets. Turn over and repeat on the back.

step 6

Bend and tuck the small flaps into the pockets. Turn over and repeat on the back.

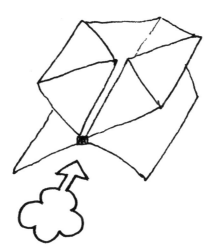

step 7

Locate the hole at the end of the model. Open up the layers of the model (this will help the model inflate) and blow into the hole.

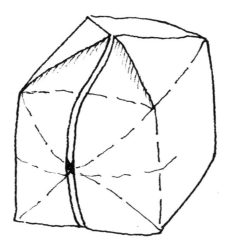

This model can be used to make beautiful origami garlands and decorations. If you fold it out of colourful, patterned washi papers, they can be threaded together with string. To do this you will need to pierce a hole in the top of the balloon opposite the blowhole and then simply thread a string through the entire model; a long threading needle might be helpful. If you use slightly translucent paper they can be placed over fairy lights and make beautiful Christmas tree decorations.

crow 烏鴉

The crow is one of the most intelligent birds in the animal kingdom. There have been studies that have shown that crows can count. They can find their way through a maze and overcome problems and obstacles in their search for food, and they are also one of the few animals that can use tools, such as sticks, to extract insects from the crevices in rotten tree logs.

Aesop's fable tells of a canny crow, dying of thirst, that comes upon a pitcher that is half full of water. When he tries to drink, his beak cannot reach far enough down to get to the water. Desperate to quench his thirst he looks around, sees some pebbles and proceeds to drop them into the pitcher. With every pebble the water level rises until finally it has risen enough that he is able to quench his thirst and save his life.

Every problem has an answer even if it might not be an obvious one. As you fold your crow, meditate on a problem you've had that you've solved in an unusual or inventive way. Often when a problem occurs we worry about it rather than think about it calmly. As we agonise, our stress level creeps up and we start to think irrationally. Mindfulness aims to allow us to think rationally in all situations and not get too caught up in the emotion of the problem. It teaches us that when we encounter a problem that we cannot solve easily we must take a step back from our emotions. We must also look at the problem with a new set of eyes.

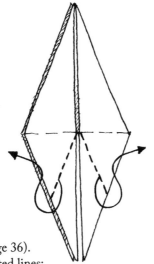

step 1

Start with a bird base (see page 36). Inside reverse fold on the dotted lines; these will create the legs. You do not need to worry about the exact angles of the fold.

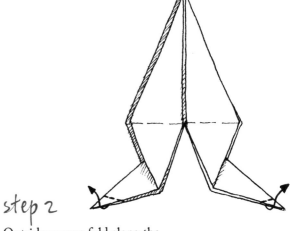

step 2

Outside reverse fold along the dotted lines to create the feet.

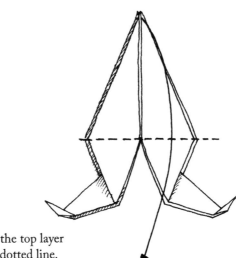

step 3

Valley fold only the top layer down along the dotted line.

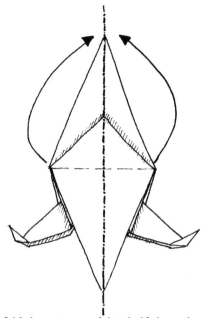

step 4

Mountain fold the entire model in half along the dotted line.

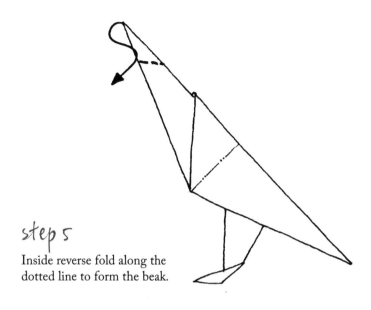

step 5

Inside reverse fold along the dotted line to form the beak.

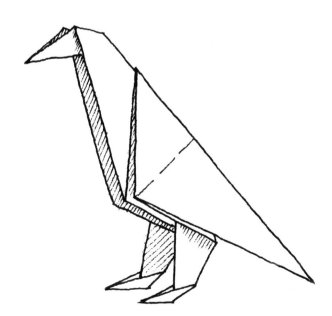

'Health is the greatest gift, contentment is the greatest wealth, a trusted friend is the best relative, nirvana is the greatest bliss.'
Buddha

gold ingot 金 元 寶

Shiny and bright, with a beautiful lustre, gold has been valued by mankind since antiquity. This model is a traditional Chinese gold ingot called a *sycee* (Cantonese) or a *yuan bao* (Mandarin). Shaped like a boat it was used as currency during the Qin dynasty and is now a symbol of wealth and good fortune; it often appears on paintings and drawings to celebrate Chinese New Year. During the celebrations, many foods are made into the shape of a *sycee* and gifted to celebrate the good fortune that comes with a new year.

Its rarity and valuable nature means that gold is often coveted; revered on account of a belief that owning a piece of the precious metal will make us happier. Yet one of life's greatest delusions is the belief that material possessions bring us happiness.

As you fold your ingot, reflect on the nature of wealth. Do material possessions really make you happy? Is true wealth the money you have in your bank account; the property and assets you own, or is it something we cannot physically hold? Of course, we all need a minimum to live but acquiring more money does not make us happier; indeed the pursuit of material gain has been the downfall of many and has led to conflict and wars. Think about the things that truly make you happy. Family, friends, fond memories, achievements, knowledge you have gained – these memories are your true wealth. The richest people are not the ones with the most gold, they are those with the most happiness.

reflections

Certain things in life are unavoidable: things break – that is a fact of life. But it is also why financial planning is necessary so that you have money saved for a rainy day. Sadness is also unavoidable, which is why I have a set of happy memories stored in case of an unhappy day. I also have a piece of music that I know calms me and an activity that I know can ease my mind of worries, even if only temporarily.

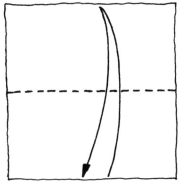

step 1

Valley fold and unfold along the dotted line.

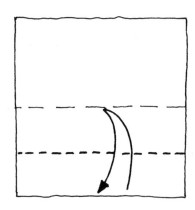

step 2

Valley fold and unfold along the dotted line.

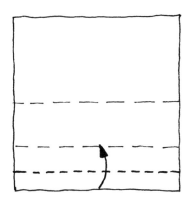

step 3

Valley fold along the dotted line.

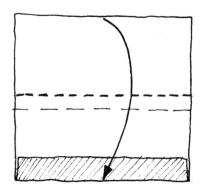

step 4

Valley fold along the dotted line to bring the top edge down to meet the bottom edge.

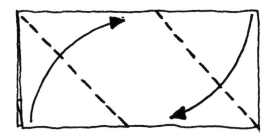

step 5

Valley fold the top right-hand corner down, then valley fold the bottom left-hand corner up. Rotate the model anticlockwise by 45 degrees.

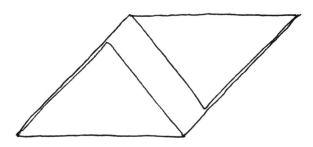

step 6

Turn the model over.

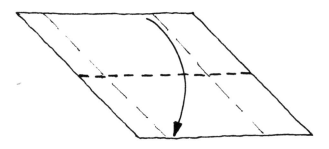

step 7

Valley fold the model in half along the dotted line. As you make this fold you will notice a triangular flap appear on the back. This is correct and will allow you to achieve the shape shown in step 8.

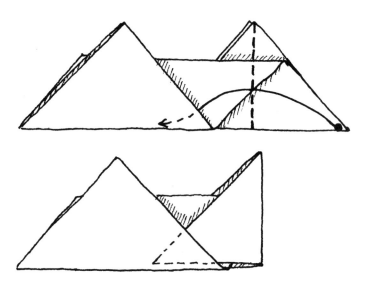

step 8

Valley fold along the dotted line, then tuck the corner under the highlighted triangle layer. Turn the model over.

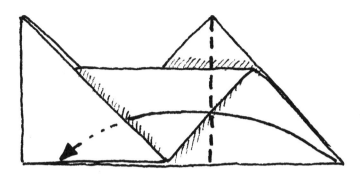

step 9

Valley fold along the dotted line and tuck the corner under the highlighted triangle layer.

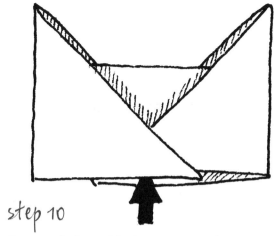

step 10

Open up the base of the ingot, separate the sides and shape the base into an oval.

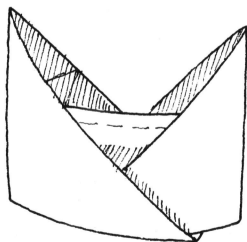

Note down your reflections as you fold.

....

....

....

butterfly 蝴蝶

Nature provides a bounty of beauties but there is perhaps none as eye-catching as the sight of a garden butterfly, its painted wings floating on a summer breeze. But besides its physical beauty, the butterfly is one of nature's most intriguing creatures. Hatched from an egg as a tiny caterpillar, it must instantly feed to grow and protect its delicate frame. After a few weeks the crawling caterpillar hides itself away in a chrysalis, to emerge, completely transformed, as a winged butterfly. Butterflies have great significance in many cultures. In Japan and Greece, for example, the butterfly is representative of the human soul; it is a symbol of rebirth and change.

In the study of chaos theory there is a concept called the butterfly effect. It was first used in weather prediction when meteorologist Edward Lorenz found that tiny changes in his forecast prediction calculations would produce vastly different results – for example the origins of a hurricane in Texas could be influenced by tiny perturbations in the system, such as a butterfly flapping its wing in Brazil. The idea is that a seemingly trivial change can have dramatic consequences.

As you fold your butterfly, consider the small changes that you could make in your life to make it happier. When we set out to improve ourselves we need to begin with small, incremental changes. If we attempt to change too much too quickly we become overwhelmed and this generally results in failure. For instance if we first start an exercise regime we do not jump directly into running a marathon; instead we start with short exercise – perhaps nothing more than 5 minutes of walking and then every day repeat and increase the duration of the exercise. The same is true for mindfulness. We cannot expect to become mindful after one session; we know that to reap the benefits we need continuous practice. You have already started by trying to become more mindful through your folding. What else can you change? Could you smile more? Be kinder?

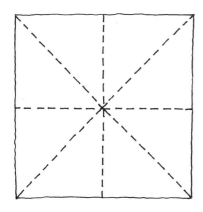

step 1

Start with an opened square base (see page 32).

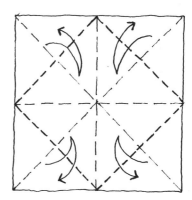

step 2

Valley fold and unfold all four corners into the middle.

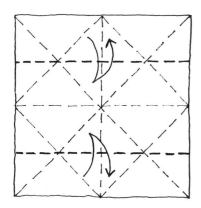

step 3

Valley fold and unfold the top and bottom edges into the middle. Then turn the model by 90 degrees and repeat the folds to give you a 4 x 4 grid of squares.

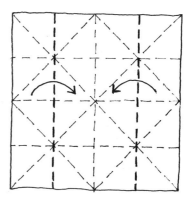

step 4

Now fold the left and right edges back into the middle.

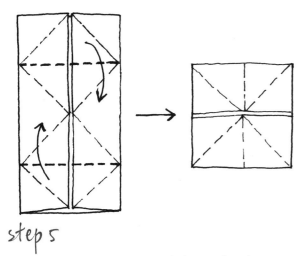

step 5

Valley fold the top and bottom halves so that they meet on the centre line, then unfold them.

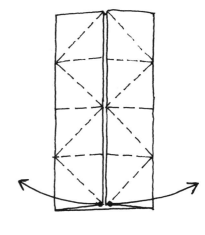

step 6

Pull out both bottom corners and valley fold along the dotted lines.

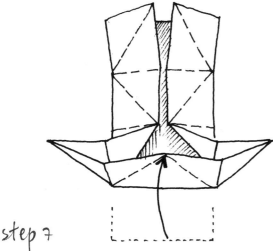

step 7

Flatten the bottom edge. Repeat steps 6 and 7 on the top half of the model.

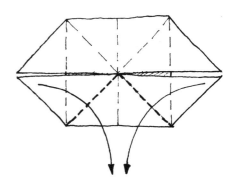

step 8

Valley fold the left and right flaps down along the dotted lines.

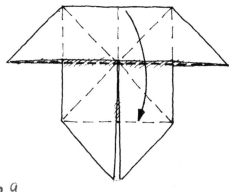

step 9

Valley fold the top half downwards along the dotted line.

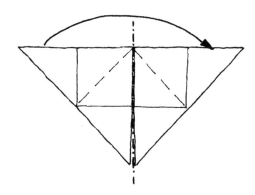

step 10

Mountain fold along the dotted line to fold the butterfly in half.

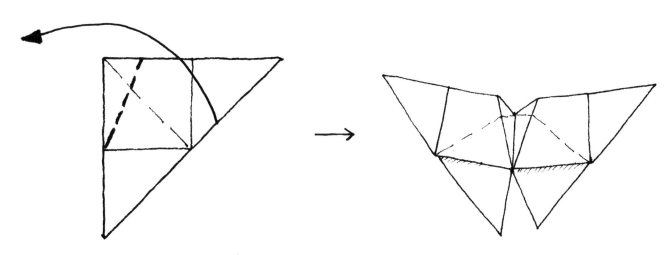

step 11

Valley fold along the dotted line (the top layer of the model only) to create the wing. Repeat on the back, then, if you want to, you can gently curl the wings.

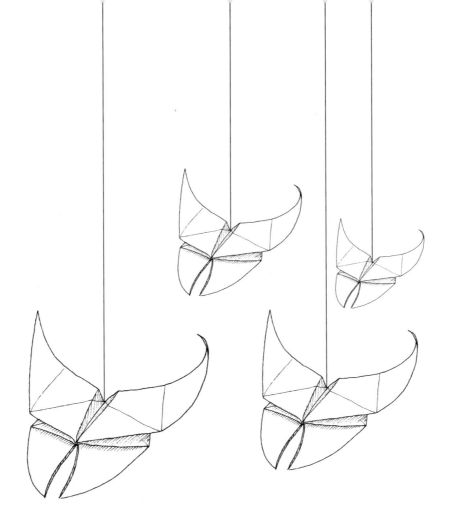

You could pierce a hole in the middle of each butterfly and hang several from a thread to make a mobile for children.

'Promise is most given when the least is said.'
George Chapman

ring 戒指

As the traditional sign of a marriage, a ring is a symbol of eternity. It is never-ending, unbroken and represents the solemn promise that two people make to love and care for each other for eternity.

As you fold this paper ring think about a promise that you have made. A promise is a declaration made to another person that you will do or not do something; it is really a request for the trust of the other person. Reflect on the nature of your promise and contemplate why it is important for you to keep it. When you break a promise, even if it seems a small or trivial matter, it is actually showing others that they cannot trust you and that you do not value your own words. The strength of any relationship is based on the level of trust between two people. If we habitually break our promises we reduce the strength of that relationship. If someone cannot trust you they cannot love you, yet to be happy we all need to love and be loved. If we are untrustworthy we will find that it is impossible for anyone to love us. And if we do not feel that we are loved by anyone we will question our own self-worth and this will negatively impact our own self-esteem and happiness. When you make a promise be sure to keep it; by keeping it you are preserving your own happiness.

reflections

I wear the wedding ring that I designed. It is made from two Möbius bands that are linked together. A Möbius band is made by taking a long strip, making a half twist and joining the two ends together to form a ring. It is a shape that has an unusual mathematical property in that it only has one side and one edge – if an ant were to crawl along it, it would end up at its starting position, having walked across the whole of the ring's surface. Engraved on one of my bands is my first initial and on the other is my wife's. The rings represent that we are two individuals with one heart and mind and that we are forever linked.

For this model you will need a piece of paper that measures 11 x 7.5cm.

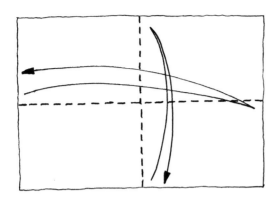

step 1

Valley fold and unfold along the dotted lines.

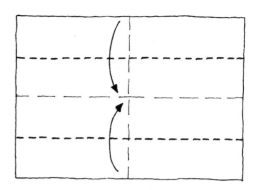

step 2

Valley fold along the dotted lines.

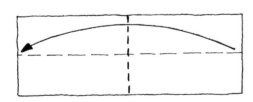

step 3

Valley fold along the dotted line.

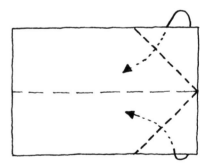

step 4

Inside reverse fold along the dotted lines.

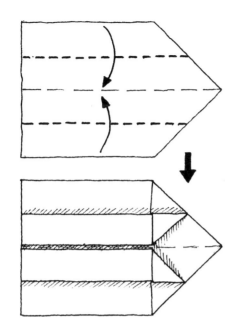

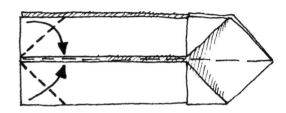

step 6

Valley fold along the dotted line on the top side only.

step 5

On the top layer only, valley fold along the dotted lines so that the top and bottom edges meet in the middle. Repeat on the back.

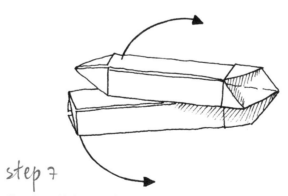

step 7

Gently pull the two flaps apart to open up the ring – you may need to put your finger inside of the square 'jewel' on the top to open it.

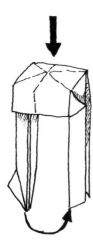

step 8

Push down slightly on the top of the ring to even out the surface. Now feed the pointed leg into the other side and tuck it in to finish the ring.

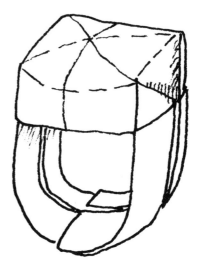

Note down your reflections as you fold.

....

....

....

....

....

'A dog is the only thing on earth that loves you more than he loves himself.'
Josh Billings

dog 狗

There are countless stories about the companionship between humans and dogs. Since its domestication, the dog's loyalty and faithfulness have earned it the title of 'man's best friend'. Family pets have been known to save lives by alerting their owners of fire, while dogs rescue people from avalanches and disasters. One story that has stuck with me was the story of a Japanese Akita dog named Hachiko. Hachiko would meet his owner Professor Ueno at Shibuya train station every day when he returned from work. In 1925 the professor died and never returned to the station where Hachiko was awaiting him, yet Hachiko continued to wait for the professor every day for nine years until his own death in 1935. In 1932 one of the professor's students wrote an article about Hachiko's loyalty and he became a national sensation. Today there is a bronze statue of Hachiko standing in Shibuya station.

As you fold your faithful friend, reflect on the nature of loyalty, friendship and trust in your own life. Consider the people to whom you are loyal. What makes them worthy of that loyalty? What qualities do you admire in them? Then think about your family, friends and the people who are loyal to you. Recognise the significant role the people we are loyal to play in our lives and the enrichment they bring. One of the most precious things in life is love and our relationships with others; appreciate the relationships you have and nurture them.

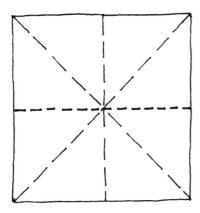

step 1

Start with an opened square base (see page 32).

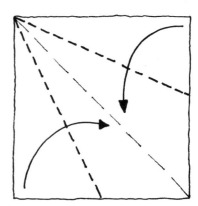

step 2

Valley fold along the dotted lines so the side edges meet in the middle.

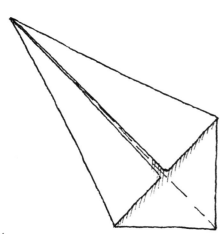

step 3

Turn the model over.

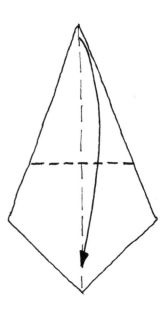

step 4

Valley fold along the dotted line so that the top and bottom tips touch.

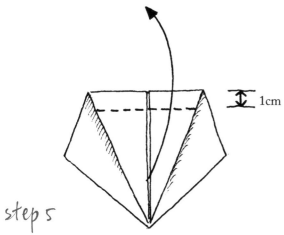

step 5

Valley fold along the dotted line.

1cm

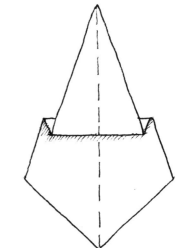

step 6

Turn the model over.

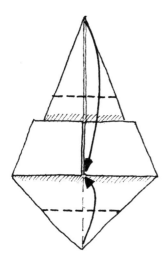

step 7

Valley fold the top and bottom tips so that they meet at the point indicated.

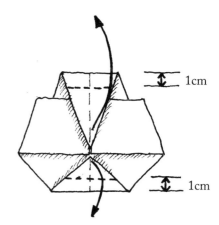

1cm

1cm

step 8

Valley fold along the dotted lines.

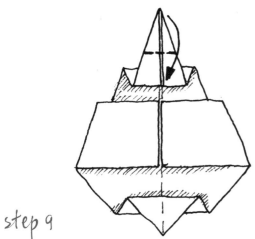

step 9

Valley fold along the dotted line.

step 10

Valley fold the model in half along the dotted line
and then rotate the model anticlockwise 45 degrees.

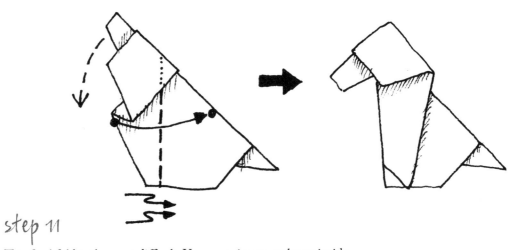

step 11

This final fold is the most difficult. You are going to make an inside
crimp fold (see page 28) along the vertical dotted line. Note that
the valley fold extends partially under what will become the head
of the dog. To do this, valley fold on the dotted line and as you
push the folds backward the head will start to swivel down.

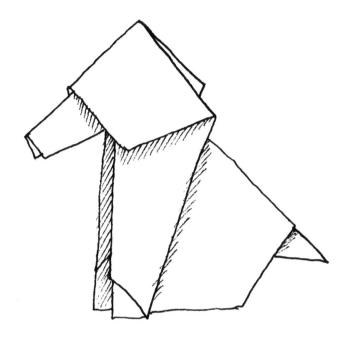

Note down your reflections as you fold.

....

....

....

....

....

dove 白鴿

The bible tells the story of Noah, who, after enduring 40 days of rain opened a window in the ark and sent out a dove to see if the water had receded. When the dove returned to him in the evening, it was carrying an olive branch so Noah knew that the water had ebbed away. Thanks to this story a pure white dove has become a universal symbol of peace and harmony: the dove with the branch in its mouth represented that heaven and earth were once again in harmony and at peace.

As you fold your dove, reflect on the nature of peace. What would peace in the world mean to you? Is there a way in which you can help to achieve this universal goal? We may feel that as individuals we are powerless to affect change but we are part of this world and we all have a part to play.

Mindfulness training is one path that can lead to inner peace. And only when every man, woman and child is at peace with themselves will there be peace in the outer world. By setting out to be more mindful and aiming to achieve your own inner peace you will be helping to create change in the world. With each person that achieves inner peace there will be one less person willing to fight, hate and wage war. With each person that achieves inner peace there will be others that will seek them out to learn from them. We are all teachers of the next generation; teach them peace and understanding and one day there will be world peace.

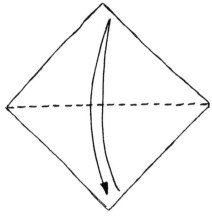

step 1

Valley fold and unfold along the dotted horizontal line.

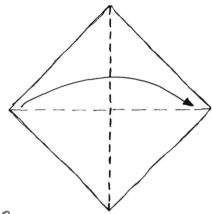

step 2

Valley fold along the dotted line.

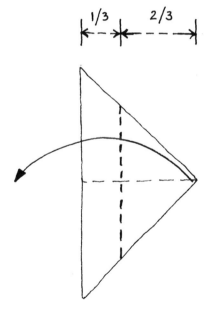

step 3

Make a valley fold approximately one third of the way in from the left.

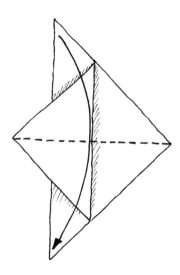

step 4

Valley fold along the dotted line.

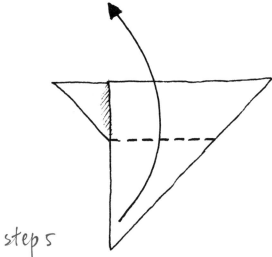

step 5

Valley fold the top layer only along the dotted line, then repeat on the back.

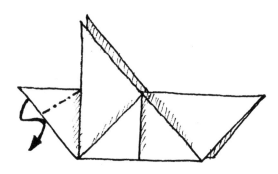

step 6

Inside reverse fold along the dotted line to form the dove's beak.

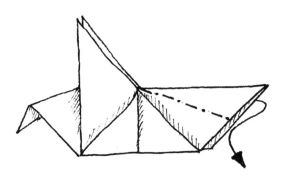

step 7

Inside reverse fold along the dotted line to start to form a tail.

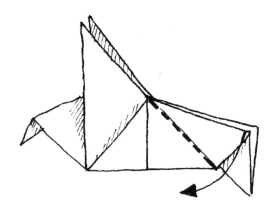

step 8

Valley fold along the dotted line on the top layer only and repeat on the back to finish the tail.

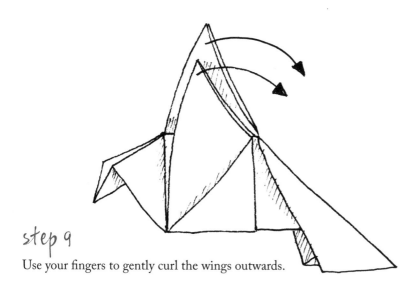

step 9

Use your fingers to gently curl the wings outwards.

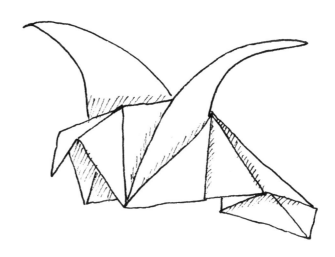

'Look up at the stars and not down at your feet. Try to make sense of what you see, and wonder about what makes the universe exist. Be curious.'

Stephen Hawking

star 星

Have you ever been lucky enough to see a shooting star? Did you make a wish? In ages past shooting stars were thought to be angels or souls travelling through heaven.

The stars have always been a source of awe and wonder but also of information. Sailors navigated the world using the celestial bodies as a map, and kings and astrologers would gaze up at the heavens and hope to divine the future from their movement.

When you look at the night sky, what do you see? We now know that these bright twinkles in the night skies are not angels or gods peering down upon us but giant fiery balls of plasma. This does not change our awe and wonderment as we stare out into space.

As you fold your paper star, marvel at the universe we live in and contemplate your own place within its beauty and its cycles. Our lives are brief, a mere flicker in the life of a star, yet they are important and precious. Regardless of whether you believe in a divine god or that our existence is down to chance, you are alive and we are all part of this universe. What we do and how we live our lives is a part of its making.

This particular model is called a lucky star and is an example of strip folding – a combination of origami and weaving.

For this model you will need a strip of paper measuring 30 x 1cm.

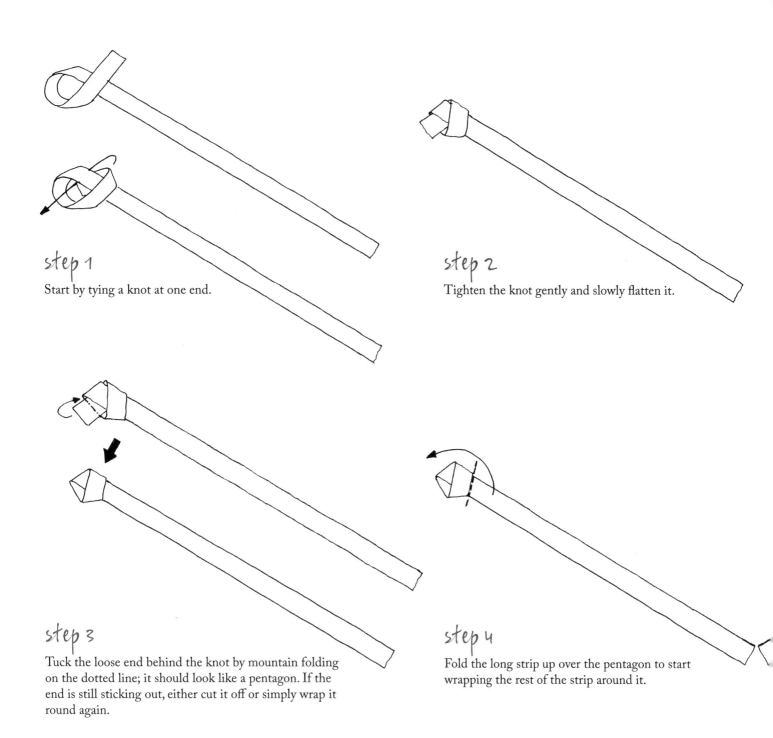

step 1

Start by tying a knot at one end.

step 2

Tighten the knot gently and slowly flatten it.

step 3

Tuck the loose end behind the knot by mountain folding on the dotted line; it should look like a pentagon. If the end is still sticking out, either cut it off or simply wrap it round again.

step 4

Fold the long strip up over the pentagon to start wrapping the rest of the strip around it.

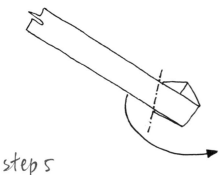

step 5

Continue to wrap the strip around the edges of the pentagon until you run out of paper.

step 6

Tuck the small end strip into the middle of the star.

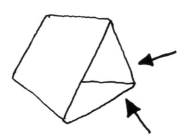

step 7

Using your finger and thumb, pinch the edges of each corner; as you do this the star will start to puff up in the centre and take on a three-dimensional shape.

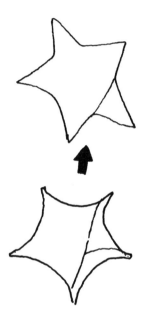

In Asia there is a custom of giving jars full of origami stars to the person you love on Valentine's Day. Often people will write messages of love on each strip of paper before they are folded up.

'A frog in a well knows nothing of the great ocean.'
Zhuangzi

frog 青蛙

In one of his most famous fables, Zhuangzi, a Daoist philosopher, tells of a frog that lived at the bottom of a well. He was born and lived his entire life there. He was very proud of his home and whenever other animals visited he would proclaim loudly that his home was the greatest in the world. One day a sea turtle came to visit. The frog invited the turtle into his home but the turtle was unable to fit through the small entrance to the well. The turtle then told the frog about his home, the sea. He said that the sea was immeasurable in depth and breadth; that the sea's volume remained constant regardless of flood or drought on the mainland. The frog was surprised, shocked and humbled at his ignorance of the world.

Often we are blinded by our own ignorance. We have superstitions and beliefs that have no basis, yet we cling to them. Some of these false beliefs manifest themselves in bigotry and prejudice that prevent us from furthering our understanding and learning. To be mindful is to have an open mind and to accept what is true and reject that which is false.

As you fold your frog, try to remember a time in your life when you had your eyes opened to a false belief. How did you feel? Were you angry? Were you humbled?

Ignorance can and often does lead to misunderstanding and intolerance. Question your prejudices and intolerances and ask if they are justified and true. Do not be a frog in a well, go out into the world, search for knowledge and different points of view. Have an open mind and be receptive to new wisdom.

reflections

I used to believe that origami was a fun but pointless skill. One day I stumbled upon a TED lecture by Robert Lang entitled 'Flapping birds and space telescopes'. Lang opened my eyes to the mathematical, scientific and medical applications of origami. He shows examples of origami being used by engineers to fold and reduce the size of large structures such as telescopes and satellite solar panels, enabling them to be sent into space. For a great insight into the practical uses of origami I highly recommend the lecture.

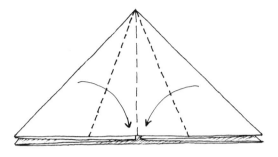

step 1

Start with a triangle base (see page 34). Inside reverse fold along the dotted lines, then turn the model over and repeat on the back.

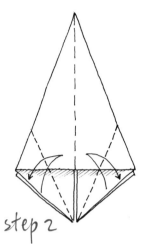

step 2

Valley fold and unfold along the dotted lines. Repeat on the back.

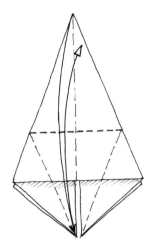

step 3

Valley fold and unfold along the dotted lines through all the layers of the model.

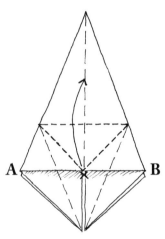

step 4

Note the position of the horizontal valley fold and the two diagonal mountain folds. Lift the point X upwards. As you lift you will notice that corners A and B will start to move towards each other. Push A and B together to meet in the middle. Point X will start to form a triangular point. Repeat on the other three sides. Please note that this model is made from a triangle base which has four branches – you will have to repeat this step four times in total.

Turn the model by 90 degrees and repeat on each branch.

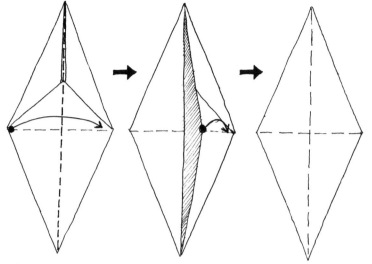

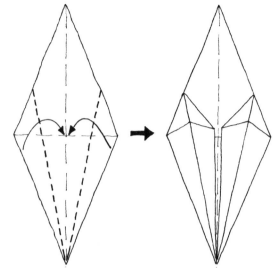

step 5

Note the triangle flap in the middle of the model. You are going to make a 'book turn' fold.

Fold just the top layer from left to right, as if you were turning the page of a book. You will be faced with a diamond shape. Repeat on the back.

step 6

On the top layer only, valley fold along the dotted line. Repeat on the other three sides.

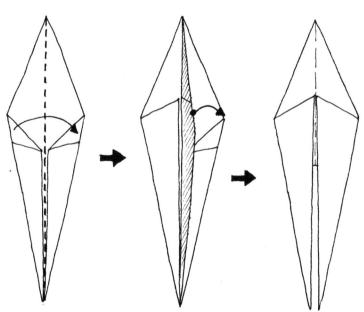

step 7

Make another book turn, then repeat on the back.

step 8

Inside reverse fold along the dotted lines to create the front legs.

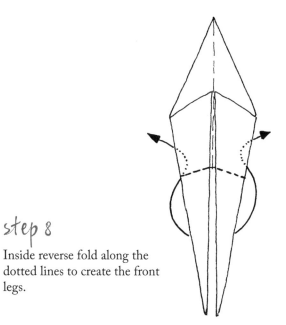

step 9

Inside reverse fold along the dotted lines to create the front feet.

step 10

Inside reverse fold along the dotted lines to create the toes.

step 11

Valley fold along the dotted line through all the layers – this forms the mouth. Turn the model over.

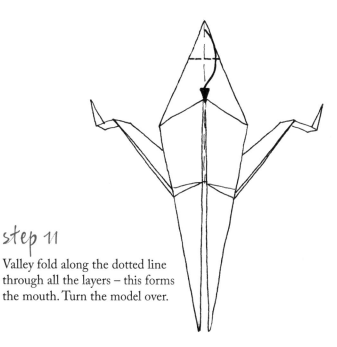

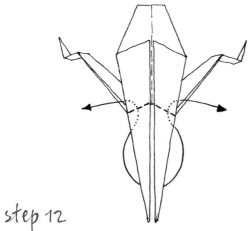

step 12

Inside reverse fold along the dotted lines to create the back legs.

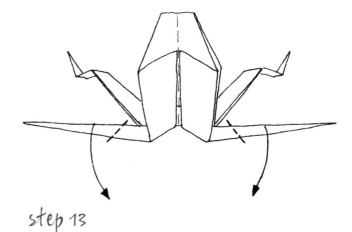

step 13

Inside reverse fold along the dotted lines to create the back feet.

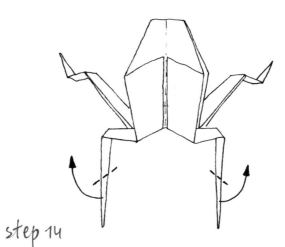

step 14

Inside reverse fold along the dotted lines to create the back toes.

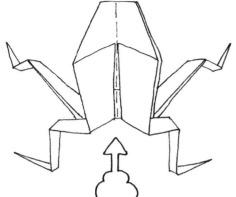

step 15

Gently blow into the back of the frog to inflate it.

Note down your reflections as you fold.

....

....

....

....

'Do not judge me by my successes, judge me by
how many times I fell down and got back up again.'
Nelson Mandela

tortoise 龜

Jonathan is a giant tortoise who lives on the island of Saint Helena in the Seychelles. He is thought to have been plodding around the undergrowth since 1882 when he arrived at the age of 50, making him around 183 years old today.

With its protective shell and long life, the tortoise and its cousin the turtle are seen as animals that are blessed by heaven and often feature in Asian creation myths. In India there is the story of Akupara the 'world turtle', who is said to carry the four elephants that support the world on its back as it travels through the universe. In Chinese mythology, the creator goddess Nüwa uses the legs of the giant sea turtle Ao to prop up the sky after the sea monster Gong Gong destroys Mount Buzhou, which had previously held up the sky.

And in western culture, the celebrated story of the speedy hare losing a race to the slow and steady tortoise never ceases to enchant and delight children due to the unexpected triumph of the underdog. It is the arrogance and complacency of the boastful hare that causes it to lose, while it is the tortoise's patience and perseverance that enables it to win what initially seems like an impossible race.

As a child, when we are learning to walk, we will often trip and fall. Sometimes the fall will hurt us and we will cry in pain. But we don't give up trying to walk – we brush ourselves off and try again and again. Through weeks and months of falling and tears we eventually learn to walk and then run and then jump and dance.

As you fold your tortoise, think back to a time when your patience and perseverance helped you achieve a goal. All talents or skills need to be practised regularly and honed. Along the way you will make mistakes but it is through determination and not being afraid of failure that we achieve success. It will be through perseverance that you will complete all the models within this book.

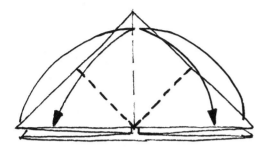

step 1

Start with a triangle base (see page 34). Valley fold and unfold along the dotted lines, then repeat on the back.

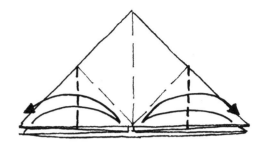

step 2

On the top layer only, valley fold and unfold along the dotted lines. Repeat on the back.

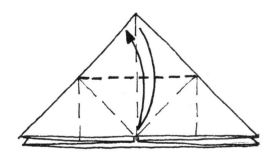

step 3

Valley fold and unfold along the dotted lines. Repeat on the back.

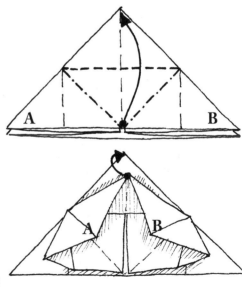

step 4

Note the horizontal valley fold and the two diagonal mountain folds. Lift up just the top layer and fold upwards. The paper will pivot along the fold lines and you will notice that corners A and B will come together and meet in the middle. This is called a petal fold. Repeat on back.

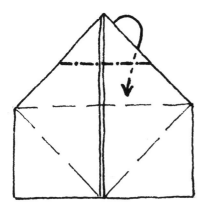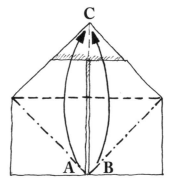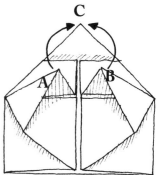

step 5

On the top layer only, mountain fold along the dotted line and tuck the flap in. Repeat on the back.

step 6

Note the position of the valley fold and mountain fold. Folding just the top layer, lift the corner A and fold it upward to the top point C. Do the same with point B. Repeat on the back.

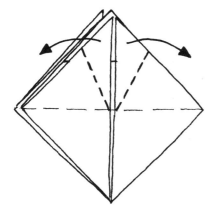

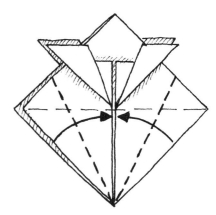

step 7

Valley fold the top layer only along the dotted line. Repeat on the back.

step 8

Valley fold the top layer only along the dotted line. Repeat on the back.

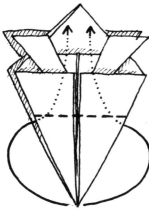

step 9

Inside reverse fold along the dotted lines.

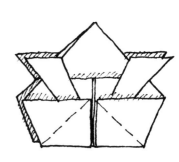

step 10

Turn the model towards you so that you are looking down at its top.

step 11

Slowly and firmly pull outwards at the points indicated. As you pull, the body of the turtle will start to puff up and round. If this doesn't happen automatically try blowing into the hole that is located on the underside of the model. This will help inflate the model and round out the shell.

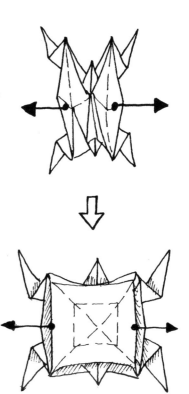

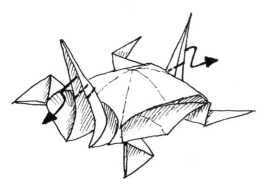

step 12

Inside reverse fold to create the mouth. Use your finger to curl the feet gently so that they are bent downwards. Note that the feet do not touch the ground in this model.

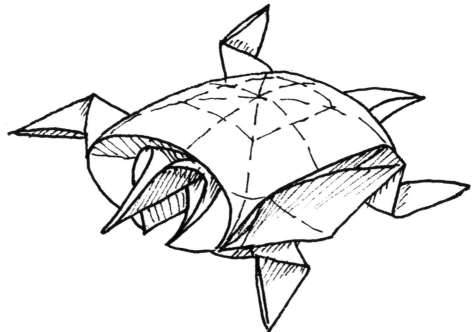

'A rose by any other name would smell as sweet.'
Shakespeare

rose 玫瑰花

Flowers have always spoken a symbolic language, communicating our thoughts and feelings in a gentle, unspoken yet implicit way. The Victorians actually developed a language of flowers, used by lovers to send romantic messages to each other encoded in the petals. Perhaps no flower has such a widely understood meaning as the red rose – the symbol of love and passion.

I created this flower for my wife Carmen and named it the Carmen rose; coincidentally my mother's Chinese name translates into English as 'rose'. This rose represents the bond between mother and child; it represents the love between me and my mother, and my wife's love for our own children.

As you fold and curl your rose, meditate on the love between a mother and child. Think about the warmth, trust, love and joy that your mother has for you or that you feel for your own children. Think about how unique and unconditional that love is and how lucky we are to benefit from a love of this kind. Allow your happy thoughts and feelings to fill your heart. Remember that everyone is someone's child and that we are all living beings that deserve to be cherished and loved. Then extend these loving thoughts and feelings towards other people – family, friends, neighbours; send them the love that you would wish for yourself. Then finally extend those feelings to someone that you have a difficult relationship with, even an enemy. With repetition this meditation will open your heart, increase your compassion and empathy and enable you to calm your mind and help resolve conflicts.

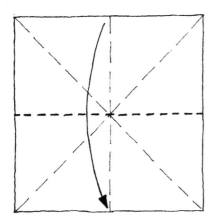

step 1

Start with an open triangle base (see page 34).
Valley fold along the dotted line.

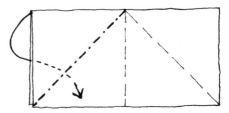

step 2

Inside reverse fold along the dotted line.

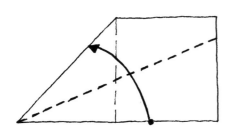

step 3

Valley fold only the top layer along the dotted
line. Note that you are folding the bottom edge
so that it lies on top of the diagonal edge.

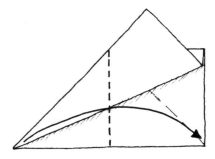

step 4

Valley fold just the top layer along the dotted line.

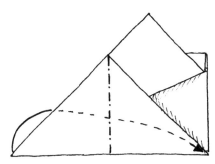

step 5

Mountain fold along the dotted line to fold the flap behind.

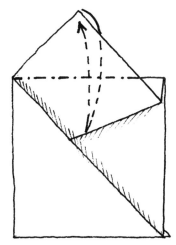

step 6

Mountain fold and unfold along the dotted line. This flap will start to form the outer petal.

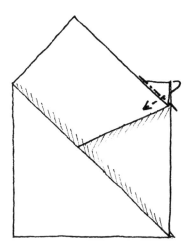

step 7

Mountain fold and unfold along the dotted line. This flap will start to form the inner petal.

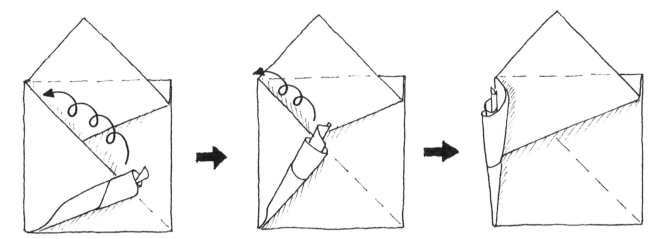

step 8

Tightly roll up the triangular flap so that it aligns with the left edge. It has to be rolled very tightly so that it doesn't unroll on its own. This will become the left curl. You may find that a pair of thin tweezers may be helpful in rolling.

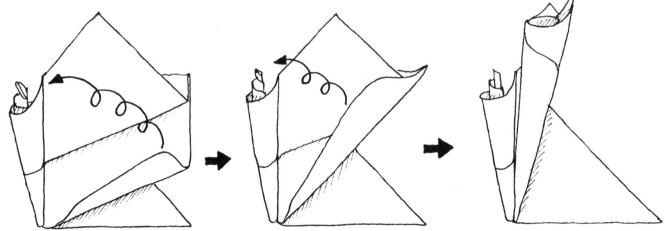

step 9

Move the left curl out of the way and then tightly roll up the main layer so it aligns with the left edge.
It has to be rolled tight enough so that it doesn't unroll on its own – this will become the central curl.

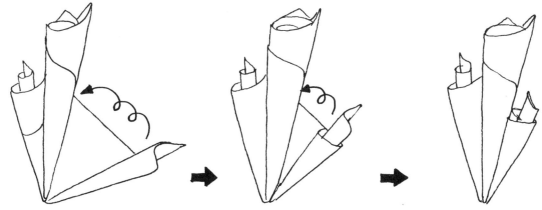

step 10

Move the central curl out of the way and then tightly roll up the last layer so it aligns with the left edge. Again, roll it tightly enough so that it doesn't unroll on its own – this will become the right curl.

step 11

This is a completed section (or unit); you will need to make five more of these to finish the rose. It's a good idea to familiarise yourself with the unit, taking a moment to note the large central curl and two smaller left and right curls.

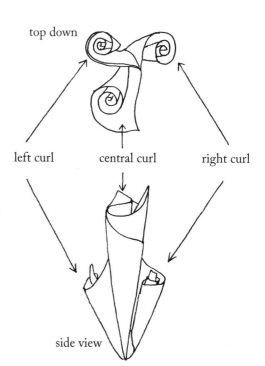

top down

left curl   central curl   right curl

side view

side view

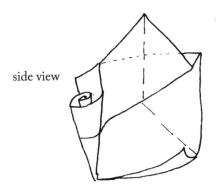

top down

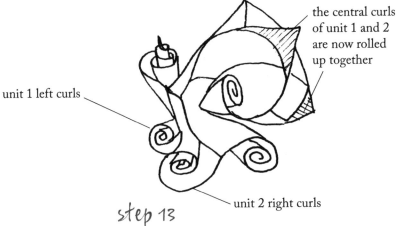

the central curls
of unit 1 and 2
are now rolled
up together

unit 1 left curls

unit 2 right curls

step 13

Using the same method as in step 12, unroll the left curl of unit 1. Unroll the right curl of unit 2, then roll them up together.

unit 1

unit 2

step 12

Once you have completed five units you can assemble the rose. First take two units and unroll the central curl on both. Lay one unrolled central curl on top of another and then roll them both back up. You will find they are now wrapped around each other.

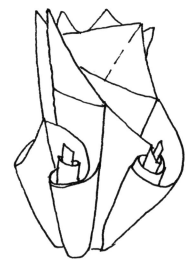

step 14

Repeat steps 12 and 13 for the remaining three until all five central curls are rolled up together and each neighbouring left and right curls are also rolled up together.

top view

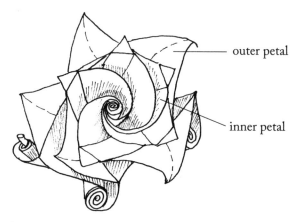

outer petal

inner petal

side view

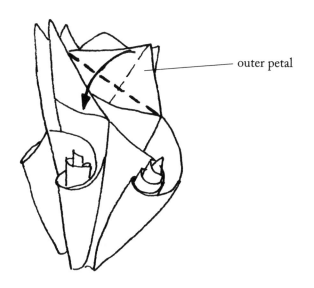

outer petal

step 15

Locate the inner and outer petals that were shown in steps 6 and 7. Fold the petals outwards and curl them with the back of your fingers to complete the rose.

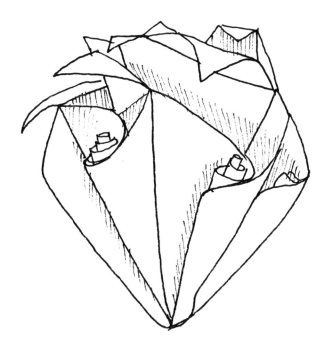

If you make 12 roses they can be joined together to form a flower ball. You can either glue or tie the flowers together with string (more advanced origami practitioners can join them using the roses' curls). Origami flower balls are referred to as *kusudama* (meaning 'medicine ball') in Japanese and were traditionally used to hold incense or potpourri. The origins of the *kusudama* are similar to a western flower pomander – spherical bouquets of scented flowers or herbs used to ward off infection and disease.

'If we fail to look after others when they need help,
who will look after us?'
Buddha

swan 天鹅

Silent and graceful as they glide across water, swans are beautiful creatures. Admired for their regal-like balletic poise, swans also mate for life and are highly protective of their young; they will not hesitate to attack would-be predators – and as such they have become symbols of love, fidelity and devotion. Swans are held in such high regard that they often appear in coats of arms alongside animals such as dragons and lions, and in the UK all mute swans are owned by the Queen and are protected by royal decree.

Perhaps the most famous story about a swan is Hans Christian Andersen's tale of the ugly duckling (see page 52), about the trials of growing up. For many, adolescence can be a turbulent time. We are burdened with the competing expectations of family, friends, peers and teachers and as we try to navigate the emotional minefield we are also undergoing huge physical and psychological changes. We all have to go through this phase and most of us have support and guidance so that we emerge as confident and level-headed individuals. But others do not and many young people suffer from low self-esteem and depression during this phase.

As you fold your faithful swan, reflect on your own adolescence. Think about the periods when you wished you had had more guidance and the people that were there for you – the family, friends and mentors that helped you overcome barriers. Now think about people in your circle. Are any going through adolescence, or just facing a difficult period in their life? Is there anybody who could benefit from a kind word, encouragement or just a call to show them that someone is thinking about them?

reflections

People practise mindfulness because it aids their search for happiness. While it is a powerful tool, I believe that to be truly content the people we care for must also be happy. We should never be so self-focused that we become unaware of others. The shortest path to happiness is to help others find theirs.

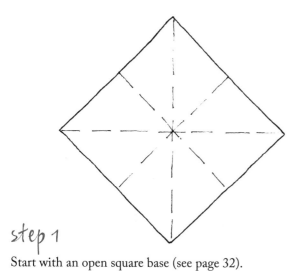

step 1

Start with an open square base (see page 32).

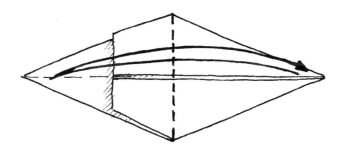

step 2

Valley fold along the dotted lines to form a kite.

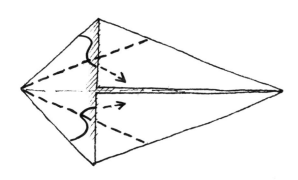

step 3

Inside reverse fold along the dotted lines.

step 4

Valley fold and unfold along the dotted line.

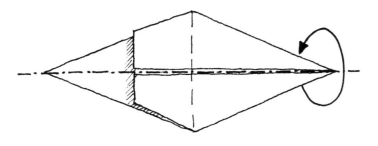

step 5

Mountain fold along the dotted line.

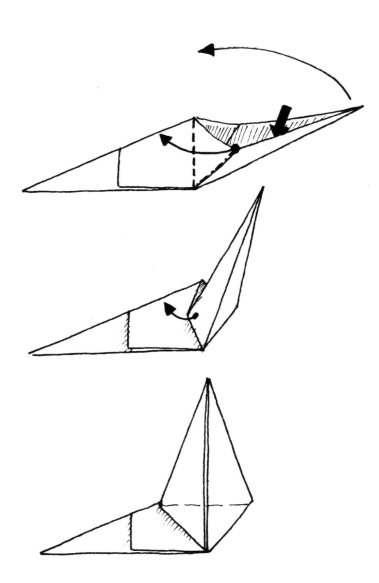

step 6

Valley fold and unfold along the dotted line.

step 7

Open up the middle of the model at the point indicated then flatten this section.

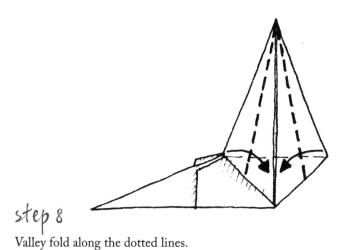

step 8
Valley fold along the dotted lines.

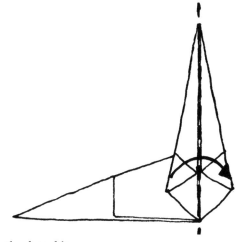

step 9
Valley fold along the dotted line.

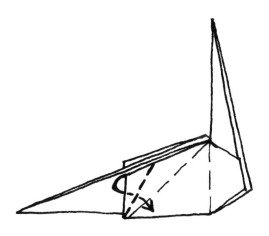

step 10
Inside reverse fold along the dotted line, then repeat on the back.

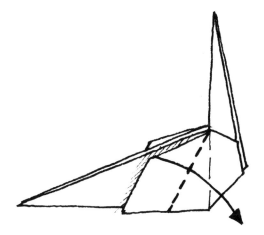

step 11
Valley fold along the dotted line (there is an existing edge that will help you make this fold). Repeat on the back.

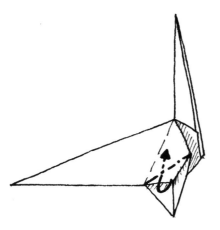

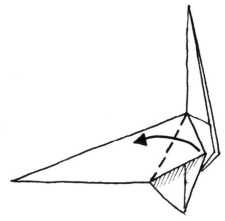

step 12

Inside reverse fold along the dotted line.
Repeat on the back.

step 13

Valley fold along the dotted line so
that the model is back to step 11.

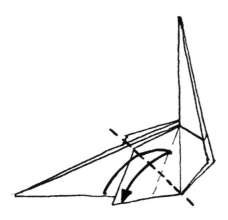

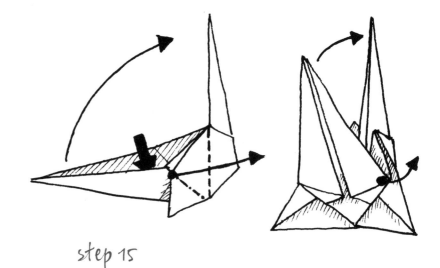

step 14

Valley fold and unfold along the dotted line
through the entire model.

step 15

The following is similar to step 7. Open up the back of
the model at the point indicated. Note the position of
the valley and mountain folds. Fold the entire back of
the model and flatten it.

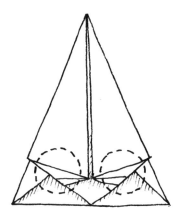

step 16

The two triangular sections that are highlighted may be slightly curved upwards. If they are, just gently flatten them.

step 17

Valley fold the top layer down along the dotted line.

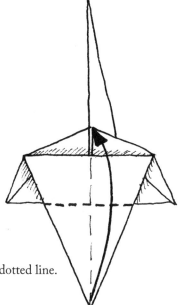

step 18

Valley fold along the dotted line.

step 19

Valley fold along the dotted line.

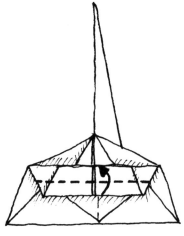

step 20

Valley fold along the dotted line. Then unfold back to step 18.

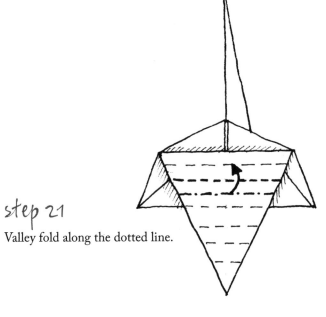

step 21

Valley fold along the dotted line.

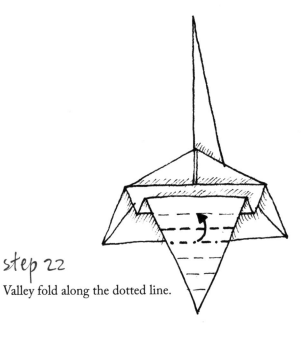

step 22

Valley fold along the dotted line.

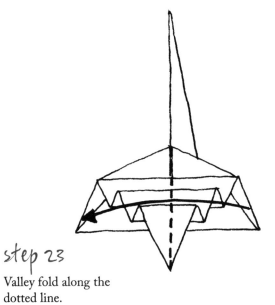

step 23

Valley fold along the dotted line.

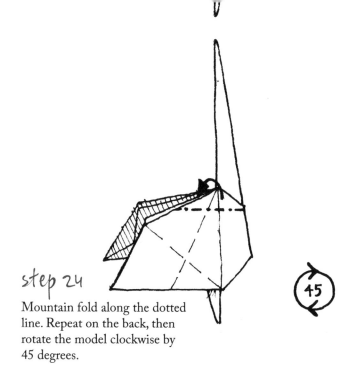

step 24

Mountain fold along the dotted line. Repeat on the back, then rotate the model clockwise by 45 degrees.

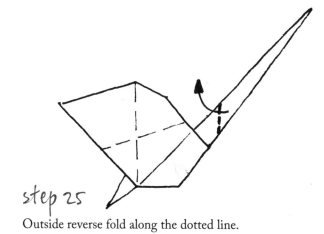

step 25

Outside reverse fold along the dotted line.

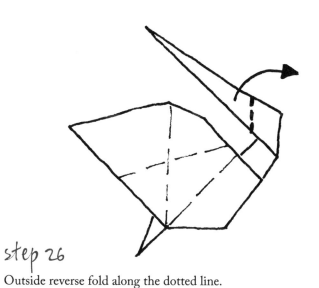

step 26

Outside reverse fold along the dotted line.

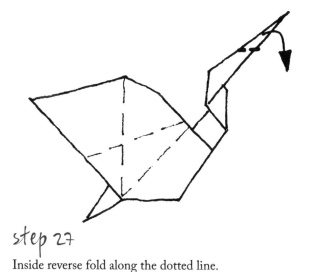

step 27

Inside reverse fold along the dotted line.

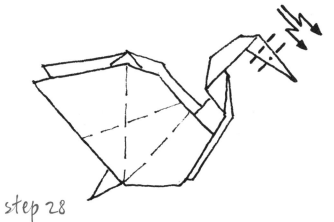

step 28

Outside crimp fold to form the beak.

step 29

Mountain fold along the dotted line. Repeat on the back to round the chest

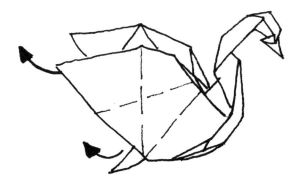

step 30

To finish the swan gently curl the tail upwards and also curl the wings so that they curve outwards and then the back tips meet.

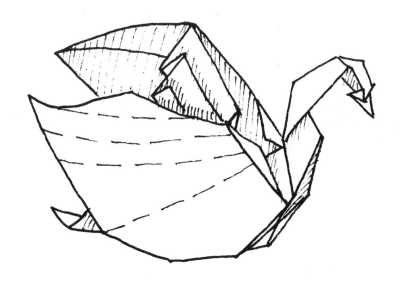

Note down your reflections as you fold.

....

....

....

....

....

'No man ever steps in the same river twice, for it is not the same river and he is not the same man.'
Heraclitus

impermanent self

You have reached the final chapter of this book. Thank you for reading the stories, making the models and meditating on their themes. I hope that you have experienced the calming, therapeutic qualities of origami.

In the last chapter of my first book, *The Book of Mindful Origami*, I asked readers to create a model that represented themselves. For this final chapter I am going to ask you to repeat the same exercise but this time to meditate on the person that you were 10 years ago. Think about the younger version of yourself and try to fold a model that represented yourself 10 years ago. Would it be the same model as the one that represents you today? Or would it be a different model?

Are you the same person you were 10 years ago? Do you have the same knowledge and perspective on life? Were you happier and wiser then or are you happier and wiser now?

The aim of this exercise is to meditate on the impermanence of our lives. As you go through life you are constantly growing, constantly changing. The person you are now is not the same as the person you were yesterday and it will not be the same tomorrow. Our thoughts, emotions and opinions alter as we acquire new knowledge, experience and wisdom. Things we once believed were true may no longer be so and vice versa. The same is true for our physical bodies; the cells in our body are constantly dividing and old cells die and give way to new cells.

By recognising that we are in motion and mutable we can appreciate that our thoughts, feelings and emotions also change. Any anger, disappointment or sorrow are just temporary experiences and if we choose to let them go they will fade away. Why linger on things that cause you distress when you can pursue things that cause you joy?

further reading

Below is a list of websites I hope you will find useful for finding out more about origami and mindfulness. If you have any questions or comments you can find me on all social media portals @mindFOLDness #mindFOLDness

general

www.mindfulorigami.com
My website where you can download crease patterns and find more information about the book. (@mindfulorigami #mindfulorigami)

www.mindfoldness.com
Focusing on developing the concepts behind mindFOLDness, the site allows you to discuss and share your models, coloured crease patterns and meditations. (@mindFOLDness #mindFOLDness)

origami

British origami society: **www.britishorigami.info**
This is a useful starting point to learn more about origami.

Origami USA: **www.origamiusa.org**
An American website with diagrams and information.

Lang origami: **www.langorigami.com**
The origami website of Dr Robert Lang, who has been a student of origami for over 40 years and is now recognised as one of the masters of the craft. It has impressive examples of advanced origami models and explains the use of origami in science and medicine.

mindfulness

www.mindful.org
A site whose purpose is to inform, inspire, guide and connect all those who want to live a mindful life, and to create a more mindful and caring society.

bemindful.co.uk
The Mental Health Foundation's guide to how mindfulness can help us all have a healthier, happier life.

www.nhs.uk/conditions/stress-anxiety-depression/pages/mindfulness.aspx
The UK's NHS page about mindfulness.

www.headspace.com
A popular mindfulness app for smartphones and tablets.

acknowledgements

This book is dedicated to the most amazing person I know, my wonderful wife, Carmen. I love you! And to the two funniest people I know, my daughters Cammy and Remy. Here is another book for your bookshelf. If you are ever stuck and don't know what to do, ask me, I will always be there.
Love Baba xx

I would like to thank all members of the Yellow Kite team. My whole family is very proud of both Mindful Origami books –they are gifts that my children will love and cherish. Thank you for creating a piece of forever happiness!

Thanks to my publisher, Liz Gough, for finding me and giving me this amazing opportunity to fulfil a life ambition. Special praise for my amazing book team, who have again produced a wonderful book in such a short time: Imogen Fortes, my editor, for giving warmth and grace to my words; Lucy Gowans, for making this book beautiful, and Richard Neal for his equally beautiful illustrations. I would also like to thank Rebecca Mundy, Caitriona Horne, Lauren Whelan, Ciara Foley and all the Yellow Kite staff for creating, supporting and promoting this book.

Thanks to all my friends who have chosen to stay by my side over the years and for all the late-night discussions about life, love, food, existence, science, philosophy, religion, champagne, Goldie's teeth, Louboutin shoes and chocolate buttons.

Thanks again to Mily Quan and Pui Fong Leung for helping to test-fold my origami models, and also Toshiko Kurata of Happy Origami Wonderland for supporting me in teaching mindful origami workshops.

Thanks to my parents, Yun Kwai Tsang and Ka-Tsun Tsang for just about everything. Thank you for all the love, wisdom and knowledge you have given me and for always being there. With special thanks to my dad for supplying the Chinese calligraphy too. Thanks to my sisters Susan and Sandra for their support and encouragement.

First published in Great Britain in 2016 by Yellow Kite
An imprint of Hodder & Stoughton
An Hachette UK company

A CIP catalogue record for this title is available from the British Library

Trade Paperback ISBN 978 1473 63502 9

Publisher: **Liz Gough**
Editor: **Imogen Fortes**
Design: **Lucy Gowans**
Illustrations: **Richard Neal**
Chinese calligraphy: **Ka-Tsun Tsang**

Printed in Spain by EstellaPrint

Hodder & Stoughton policy is to use papers that are natural, renewable
and recyclable products and made from wood grown in sustainable
forests. The logging and manufacturing processes are expected to
conform to the environ¬mental regulations of the country of origin.

Hodder & Stoughton Ltd
Carmelite House
50 Victoria Embankment
London
EC4Y 0DZ

www.hodder.co.uk

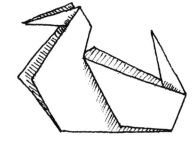

'Shape clay into a vessel; it is the
space within that makes it useful.'
Lao Tzu

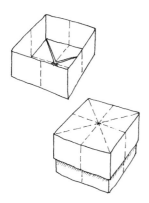

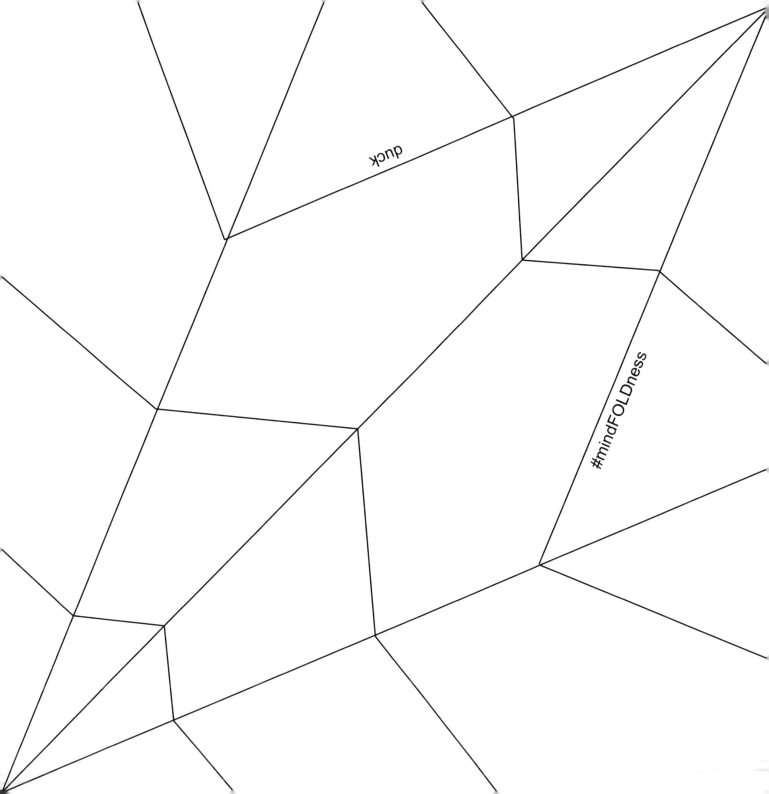

'Prejudice is a burden that confuses the past, threatens the future and renders the present inaccessible.'

Maya Angelou

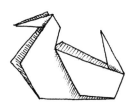

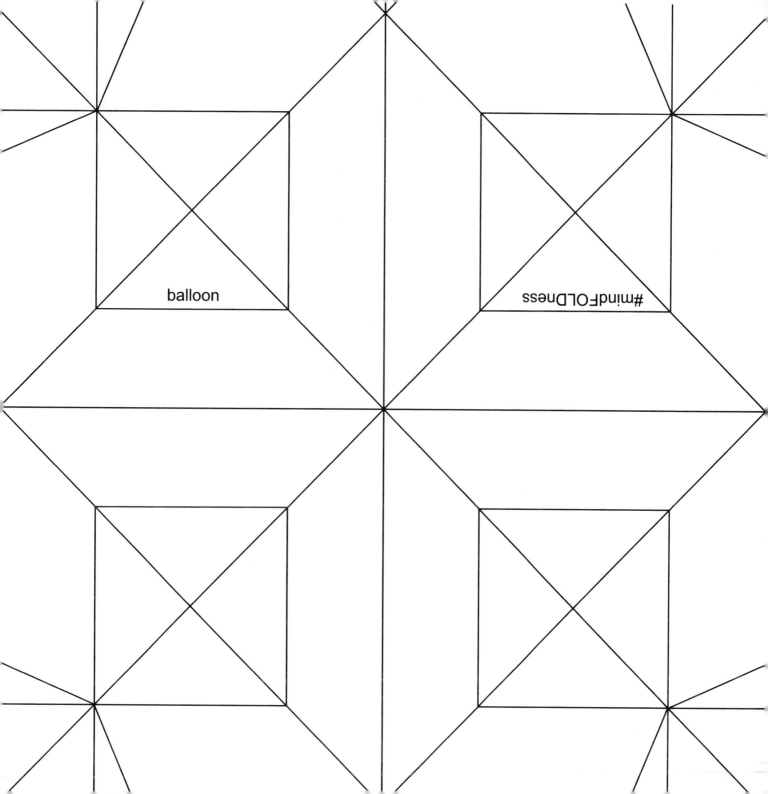

'All men know the use of the useful, but nobody knows the use of the useless.'
Zhuangzi

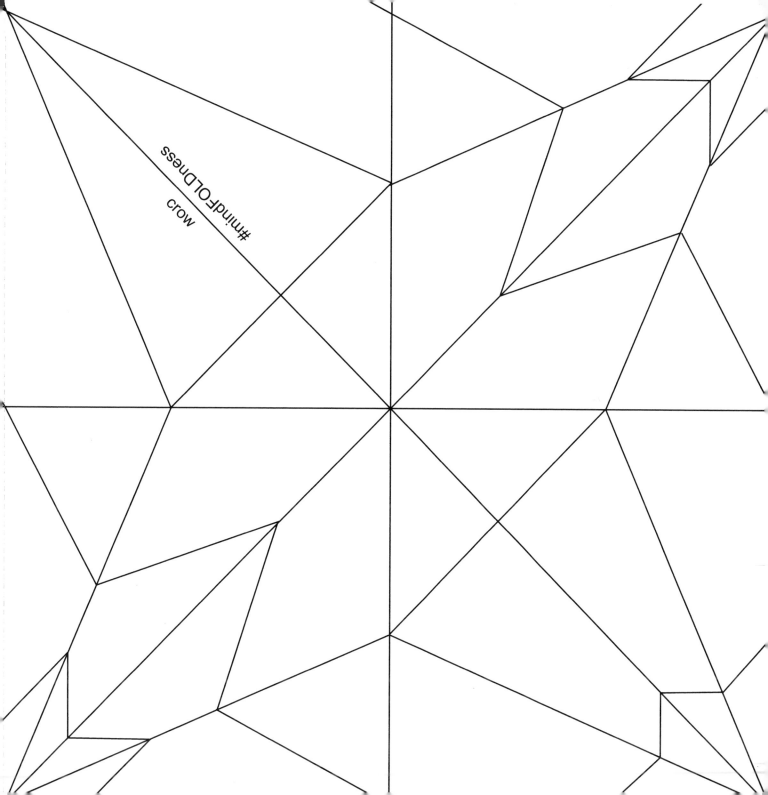

#mindFOLDness
crow

'Necessity is the mother of invention.'
English proverb

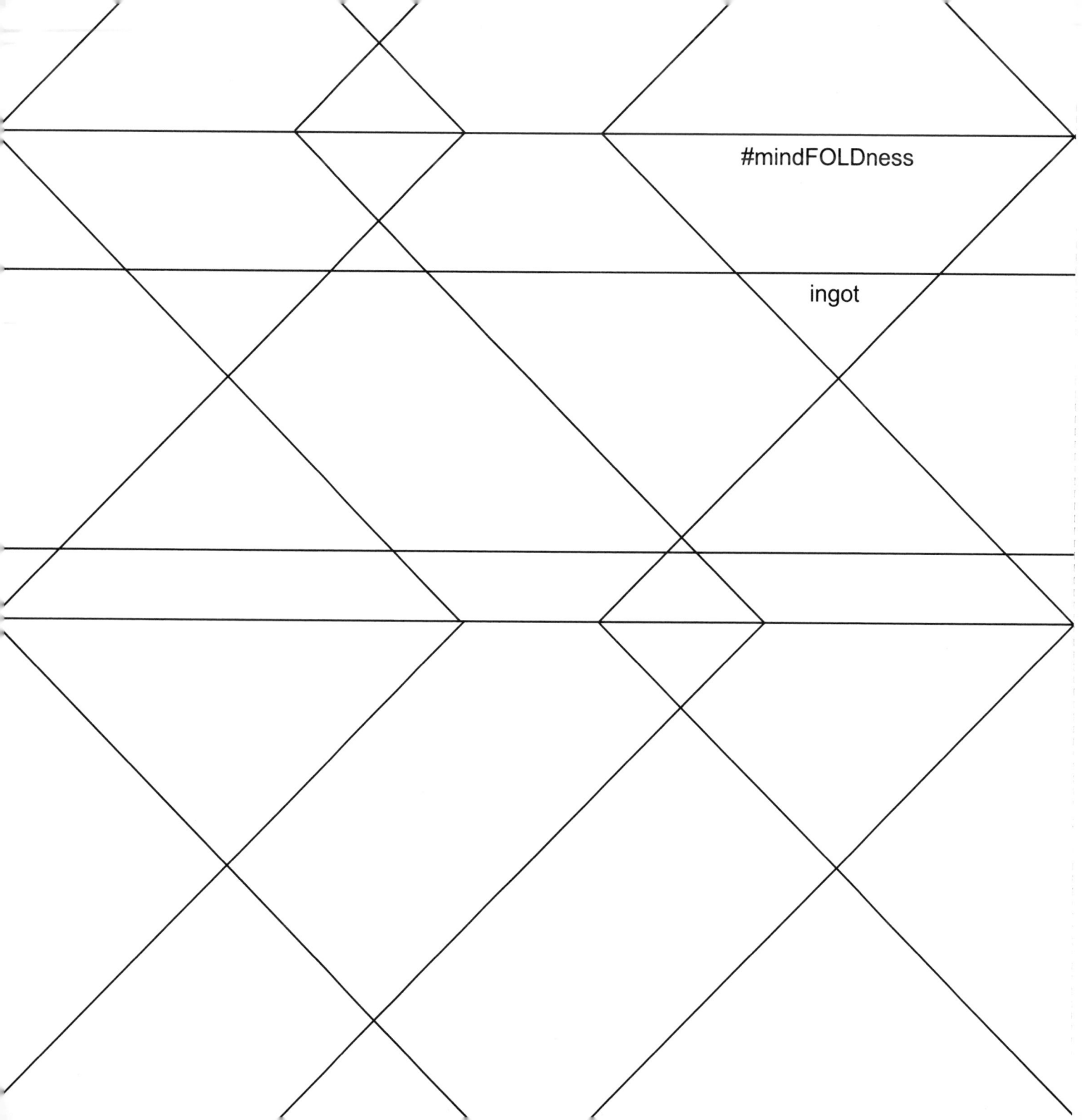

#mindFOLDness

ingot

'Health is the greatest gift, contentment is the greatest wealth, a trusted friend is the best relative, nirvana is the greatest bliss.'
Buddha

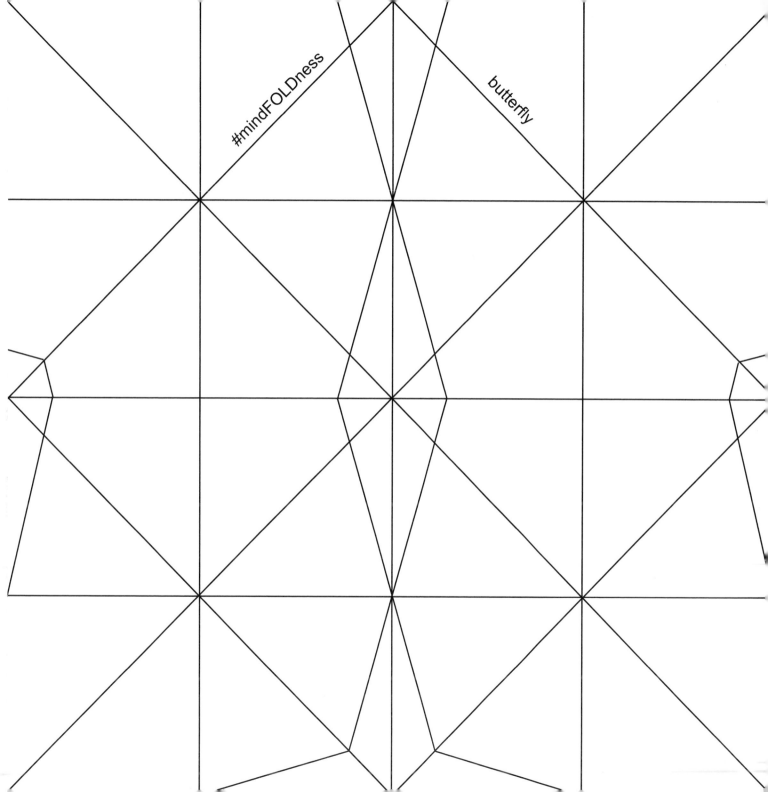

'If nothing ever changed there would be no butterflies.'

Unknown

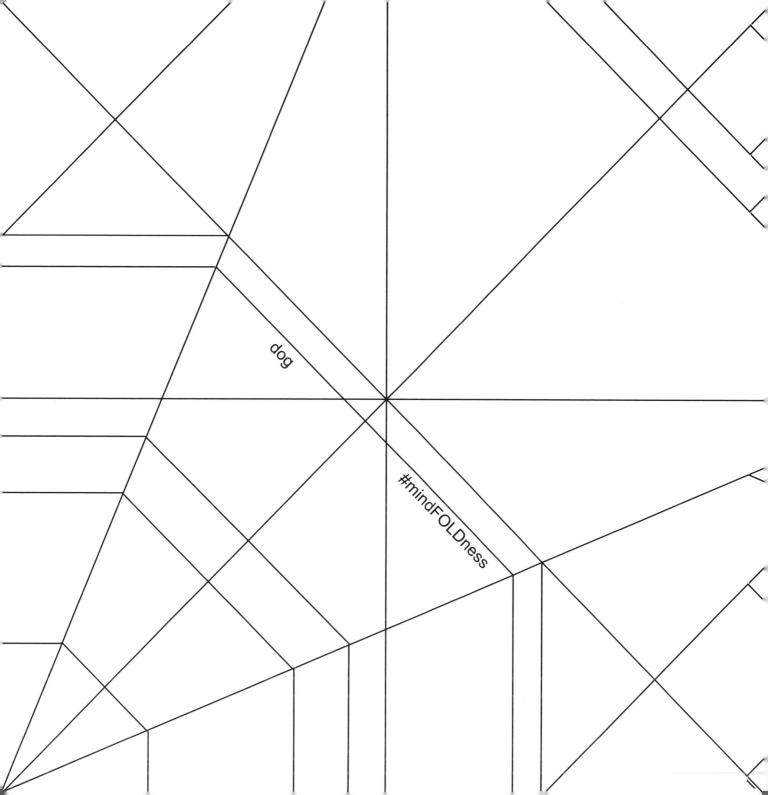

'A dog is the only thing on earth that loves you
more than he loves himself.'
Josh Billings

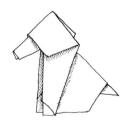

#mindFOLDness   frog

'A frog in a well knows nothing of the great ocean.'

Zhuangzi

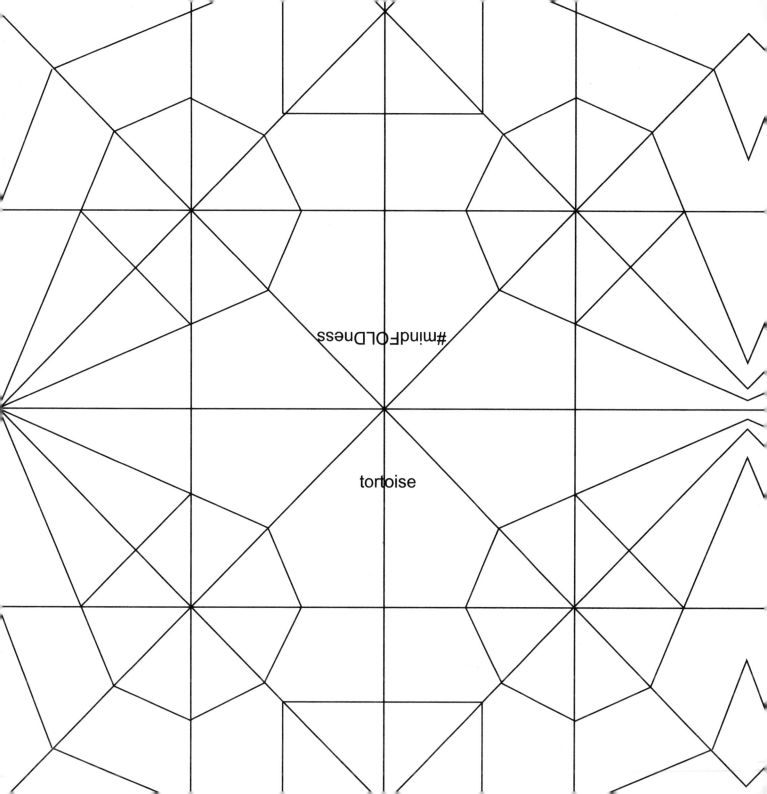

#mindFOLDness

tortoise

'Do not judge me by my successes, judge me by how many times I fell down and got back up again.'

Nelson Mandela

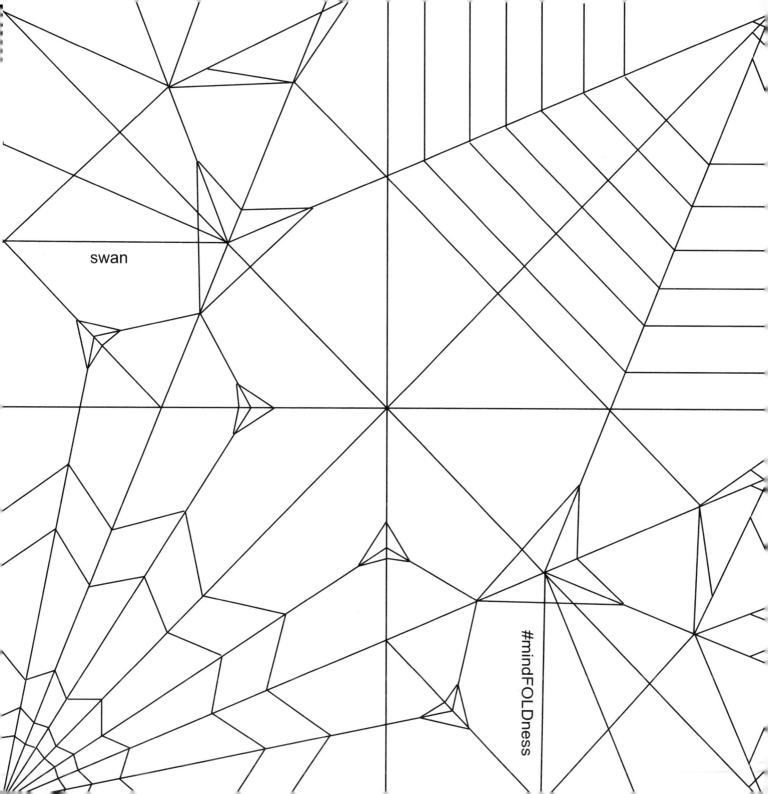

swan

#mindFOLDness

'If we fail to look after others when they need help,
who will look after us?'
Buddha

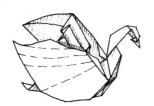

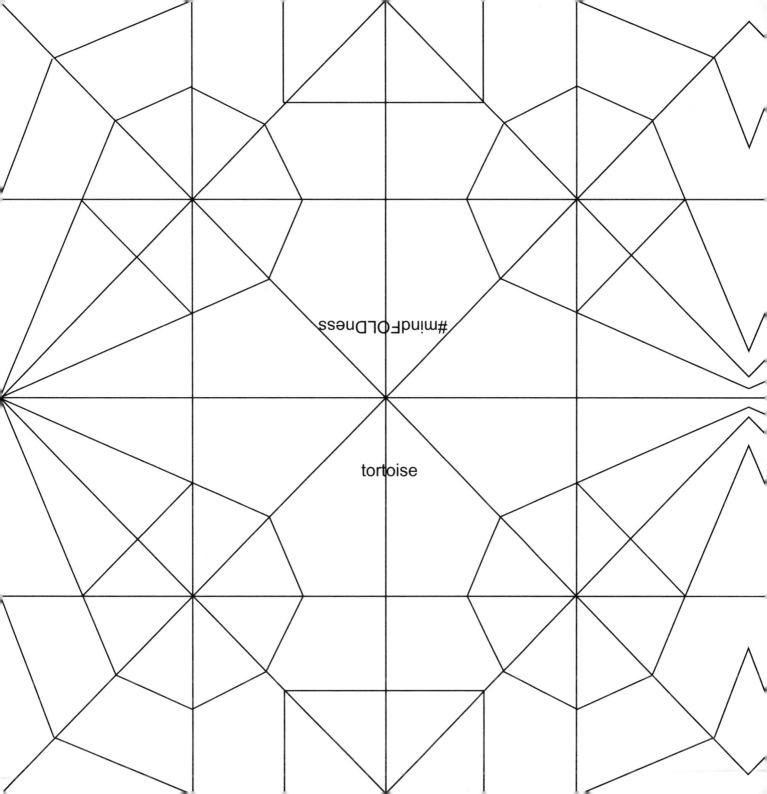

#mindFOLDness

tortoise

'Do not judge me by my successes, judge me by
how many times I fell down and got back up again.'
Nelson Mandela

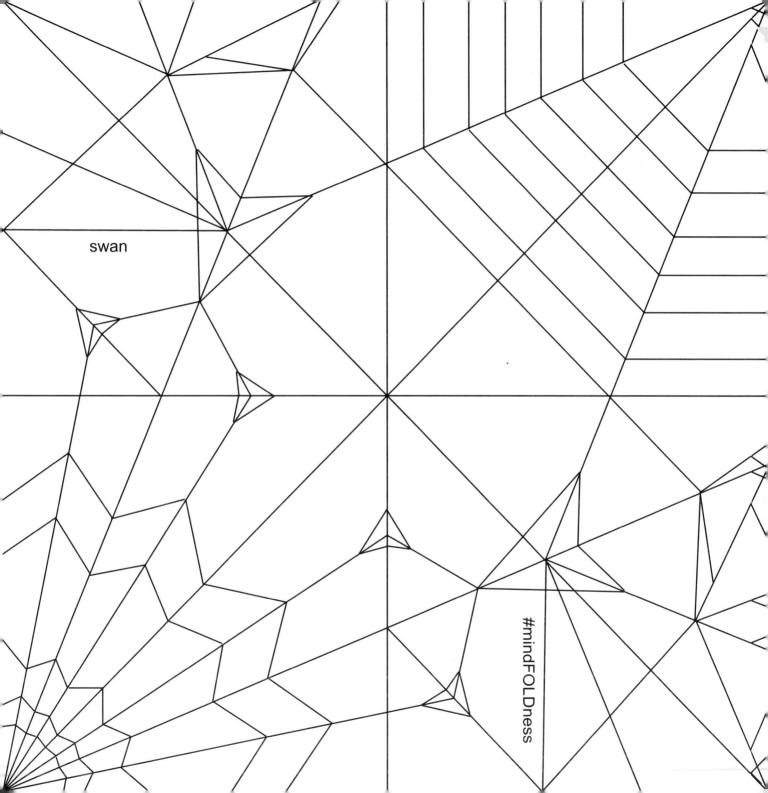

'If we fail to look after others when they need help, who will look after us?'

Buddha